The Bible as Prayer

For my mother

The Bible as Prayer:
A Handbook for *Lectio Divina*

Stephen Hough

PAULIST PRESS
New York/Mahwah, N.J.

This edition published by arrangement with
Continuum
The Tower Building
11 York Road
London
SE1 7NX

ISBN 978-0-8091-4507-2

Library of Congress Cataloguing-in-Publication Data:
A catalogue record of this book is available from the Library of Congress

Published in 2007 by
Paulist Press
997 Macarthur Boulevard
Mahwah, New Jersey 07430

Typeset by BookEns Ltd, Royston, Herts
Printed in China by 1010 Printing International Ltd

Contents

Rabbi Zusya of Hanipol once started to study a volume of the Talmud. A day later his disciples noticed that he was still dwelling on the first page. They assumed that he must have encountered a difficult passage and was trying to solve it. But when a number of days passed and he was still immersed in the first page, they were astonished, but did not dare to query the master. Finally one of them gathered courage and asked him why he did not proceed to the next page. And Rabbi Zusya answered: 'I feel so good here, why should I go elsewhere?'

Abraham Joshua Heschel, *The Earth is the Lord's: The Inner World of the Jew in Eastern Europe* (Woodstock, VT: Jewish Lights Publishing, 1995)

Introduction

Why? The Background

Often, when reading a book or an article on prayer and the spiritual life, I have come across a list of biblical phrases, suggested by the author, as material on which to meditate. What I wanted to do with *The Bible as Prayer* was to take a comprehensive collection of extracts from the Scriptures which I thought could be used in this way, and to list them in chronological order – to take all the cherries out of the cake, to present the diamonds already mined, in a neat pile, so that one's own devotional jewellery could be created without having to chip away at the rock. And I hope too that the gems which follow here, one after another, will encourage the reader to return to their context with renewed interest and reverence.

The Bible as Prayer is a resource to use, an anthology for the busy person to keep at hand in a pocket or briefcase, enabling them to focus on the business of prayer straightaway. It is absolutely not meant to replace the Bible of course, but rather to make its most luminous phrases more easily accessible, facilitating its use for contemplative prayer. Everything has a devotional not scholarly purpose, and as such it is intentionally limited. All the extracts, although in chronological order, are designedly out of context, but only in the way they would be if we were to take a favourite verse or passage from the original to mull over and savour; indeed the Bible quotes itself out of context in numerous places for both devotional and didactic purposes. This book also has an ecumenical dimension: it draws on both Eastern and Western monastic traditions; around half of the text is from the Jewish scriptures; and it should not be forgotten that it was the churches of the Reformation which first taught us to take the vernacular Bible into our hands and hearts.

How? The Methods

Nobody is an expert in prayer. A sense of helplessness, of inadequacy, or even failure, is the first step – every time – to opening our hearts to the One who prays in us.[1] Any 'success' in prayer is measured by our intention. To *want* to pray, even with reluctance, and to make time for the attempt, *is* to pray. 'Wasting time with God' is how one writer put it. But if I can risk making some specific suggestions about a subject best experienced in silence I would highlight three ways in which this book can be used:

1. *Lectio divina* (the Benedictine method)
2. Jesus Prayer – vocal prayer (Eastern Orthodox method)
3. Affective aspirations

These three ways have in common an aim to reduce Scripture to one phrase or idea when praying. Early in the monastic traditions of both East and West, monks, aiming to pray constantly (following St Paul's injunction: 'Pray without ceasing'),[2] would take a short phrase and repeat it over and over again. The words themselves were merely a gateway into the presence of God through which we were meant to pass, beyond intellectual concepts, into filial conversation and intimacy, reduced in the end to silence or inner rest – 'hesychia' as it was known in the Eastern churches. In the West this would most often be a line heard during communal devotions which the monk would then take back to his cell on his lips and in his heart; not so much meditating through reading as: listening … remembering … repeating. In the East, particularly from the fourth-century Desert Fathers onwards, short prayer-formulas would be repeated ceaselessly, crystallizing over many centuries into what became known as the Jesus Prayer: 'Lord Jesus Christ, Son of God, have mercy on me'.[3]

---

1. Rom. 8: 26.
2. 1 Thess. 5: 17.
3. Sometimes the words 'a sinner' are added at the end of the prayer.

INTRODUCTION

Lectio Divina

This ancient way of praying, originating it seems in the monasteries of the Egyptian desert, fell into disuse for many centuries when more elaborate methods were in fashion in the Roman Catholic Church. After the Reformation, zealous spiritual directors, particularly in the many new religious orders springing up, found forms of *lectio* too loose and open to abuse, and they tried to create foolproof formulae for mental prayer, much like fitting a brace to prevent teeth from growing out of shape. The complexity of these methods risked making prayer into a form of mental gymnastics, with the added danger of pride for those who won the prize.[4] Yet even by the sixth century, St Benedict in his Rule (written *c.* 530 CE) was already advising his monks to spend up to three hours a day doing *lectio* – a significant change from earlier, simpler methods, and an insurmountable obstacle for those with no access to books or for those who couldn't read, both inside and outside the monasteries. The ensuing, unavoidable separation between lay and clerical states was a major bone of contention for the sixteenth-century Reformers, and it persisted in Catholic religious life right up to the Second Vatican Council. Since the Council, with its windows opening to the distant past as well as to the secular present, there has been an enthusiastic rediscovery of more ancient methods of devotion. Theologians have been excavating and exploring the riches of their own and other's traditions. However, even today there is still the danger of writers making the inspirational into the institutional. With all good intentions, we try to pin something down; we put a frame around it, glass in front of it, and hang it on a wall, whilst the real contemplative 'butterfly' is flying freely in the fields. We weave a web of complexity which can be beautiful, even perfect in design, but which can also entangle and strangle. For the simpler spiders amongst us a single thread should be enough to attach us to God.

---

4. A glance at some of the volumes of ascetical and mystical theology from the past few
    hundred years is to behold something magnificently yet often bewilderingly intricate.

3

Despite its name, *lectio divina* is not spiritual reading or Bible study as such. Those involve using the intellect to dissect, absorb and store theological ideas; and, excellent as they are in themselves, can be a distraction to the work at hand in *lectio* which is communion with God. The sooner a book can be put aside and the affections stirred when praying, the better. Indeed one of the chief purposes of the present book is to minimize the temptation to turn the time of *lectio* into a reading session.

The classic description of the method is as follows:

Lectio – *reading*
We settle down in the presence of God and take up a book of spiritual reading. The Scriptures have an obvious priority.

Meditatio – *reflection*
When we find an attractive phrase or sentence we stop, going over and over it in our minds. Thinking about the actual meaning should only be the beginning: we should try to 'taste' the words, repeating them lovingly until they sink deep into the heart and soul. We may eventually find ourselves reducing the sentence to one word above the others.

Oratio – *response*
The act of *reflection* should lead us freely and confidently into conversation with God. We speak to God.

Contemplatio – *rest*
We leave behind words and concepts and simply rest in the arms of our Father in peace and childlike trust. God speaks to us.

The beauty of this method is that we are never really wasting our time as long as we try not to shorten the time decided upon (twenty minutes is a commonly suggested minimum) and keep within the cycle of these four activities. Sometimes it will be easy and within seconds an inspiring phrase will lead us immediately into intimacy with our Creator; at other times we'll have to keep returning time and time again to the written text. However, this whole system should only be a guideline and can be seen either as a hierarchical series of stepping stones or, as Fr Thomas Keating has suggested, four points on the circumference of a circle, all of which are related to the centre, which is God speaking to us through His word.

The main things to guard against are that:

1. the *Lectio* does not become mere curious reading;
2. the *Meditatio* does not become mere distracted thoughts;
3. the *Oratio* does not become an endless monologue on our part;
4. and that the *Contemplatio* does not send us to sleep!

There will be as many ways of doing this as there are people praying. One way of using a pregnant biblical text for meditation is given by Fr Richard Rohr[5] in the following example from Psalm 46:

> Be still and know that I am God
> Be still and know that I am
> Be still and know
> Be still
> Be

Lectio can also be done in a group setting, especially on a retreat or at a conference when there is time. Someone can read out aloud one of the phrases and then leave a sufficient gap for meditation. In the new *Anglican Common Worship: Daily Prayer* (2005) the liturgy for 'Prayer During the Day' contains a specific space for this in its 'Response' section.

Jesus Prayer (vocal prayer)

This is in a certain way a variation on the first method, but with more emphasis on the actual repetition of the words. It doesn't

---

5.   Richard Rohr OFM, *Everything Belongs* (Edinburgh: Crossroad Publishing Co., 1999).

literally have to involve the vocal chords and can be silent, but the phrase should remain in the foreground in a way that it needn't with *lectio*. Where the latter is merely a springboard to dive into deeper conversation with God, vocal prayer is more like a recreational promenade by the ocean where we remain for the duration of our prayer, 'walking' up and down the phrase chosen, enjoying the water from different vantage points. We can take a phrase (any of the shorter ones from this book will do) and treat it almost as a mantra. The Jesus Prayer itself ('Lord Jesus Christ, Son of God, have mercy on me') is central to Eastern Orthodox spirituality, and its history takes us back to the earliest years of the Christian era. Although this specific formula does not appear until about the sixth or seventh centuries, St John Cassian (*c.* 360–435 CE) writes in his *Conferences* that the monks of the Thebaid (whose community dated from the third century) would repeat the words, 'O God come to my assistance; O Lord make haste to help me'[6] throughout the day and always. Later writers explored ways of making such prayer not only constant, but involving the use of the entire body. It could be timed with breathing in and out as if a heartbeat, or punctuated with genuflections and prostrations; it could be synchronized with walking, and on pilgrimages recited out aloud whilst undergoing the arduous journey. The prayers could also be counted with stones or beads, out of which practice developed the Rosary in the West and the prayer rope in the East – ways for the illiterate to have an equivalent religious practice to the chanting of psalms in Latin in the monastery choirs.

So we can take any of the shorter extracts from *The Bible as Prayer* and repeat them as the monks in the earliest centuries did: on our fingers, with beads, with our breathing, or simply as we walk to the office. As we repeat the phrase we can linger on, or focus on different words each time. The following example, from Psalm 23, is one way this could work:

---

6.   Psalm 70: 1.

The Lord Is My Shepherd

The Lord ... *Who is the Lord? The Creator of all, the Father who loves us and holds us in being. Not a Lord but the Lord;*

is *– not was, or will be. The present moment is the only place where we exist and where God exists: everything else is fantasy;*

my *– not an anonymous, generalized relationship, but a personal contact;*

Shepherd *– one who takes care, who protects, feeds, watches, guides, cherishes, and is responsible for the sheep.*

Affective Aspirations

This is an even simpler, less structured method than the other more venerable ones: we simply take the book, take a point, and take it away – like popping a sweet into our mouths, or keeping a catchy tune under our breath. No pressure, no expectations, just a phrase that will please or console, which we allow to rest almost superficially in the mind alongside the busyness of the day or the exhaustion of the night. Indeed, at those times when circumstances prevent us from praying (leaving the house late, meetings all day, a social event in the evening) a phrase can be taken in the car or on the train and gently repeated in place of more formal prayer.[7] When someone is ill this might be all they can manage. Certain phrases can become reflexes which transform our lives: 'My soul finds rest in God alone'[8] can be most soothing after a hard, frustrating day; 'Be still and know that I am God'[9] can kick in automatically when worries and agitation threaten to overwhelm us; 'Thanks be to God' can roll off the tongue dozens of times a day with the countless blessings we receive, most of which we ignore or fail to notice. It can also be used in times of pain and disappointment when we realize that 'All things work together for good for those who love God'.[10] But everything

---

7. St Francis de Sales even suggested this concession with his characteristic leniency and understanding.
8. Psalm 62: 1.
9. Psalm 46: 10.
10. Rom. 8: 28.

with simplicity and freedom: anxiety, scruples and obsessions are dangers always lying in wait for us in any religious practice.

It can be seen that all of the above methods and examples overlap and intertwine in a sort of 'devotional ecumenism' – wistfully reminding us of the era when the early Church was taking its first breaths with both youthful lungs. In the West the selection of a simple phrase led to a contemplative reading of numerous texts; in the East the selection of a simple phrase became fixed into *one* form and spawned its own vast literature of contemplation. *The Bible as Prayer* attempts to leapfrog across the divisions and beyond the techniques to the simplicity and flexibility of the earliest Christian centuries. One day the phrase we select may be more fruitful in the mind, another day on the lips, and another day in the heart. It is all the same to the God who has already chosen and redeemed us, and for whom prayer should simply be a way for us to take time to relish who we are – His beloved sons and daughters.

What? The Text

The Bible (the word means 'book' in Middle English) is not a book, but a collection of books – a precious, sprawling, uneven library rather like a patchwork quilt. Some squares are so familiar that they have almost lost their pattern or colour; others are so little read that they are musty and stiff; and it appears that still others have been lost or removed at an earlier point in history, rejected by the Church Fathers who sewed these particular squares into this particular quilt. It is perhaps the most sold yet least read book of all time; the most quoted, yet least observed. Useless lists of unknown, unremarkable people following obsolete laws, buried in an alien desert under the sands of history, lie next to names which resound by the minute in the lives and surroundings of almost every culture on earth: Jesus Christ, King David, Abraham, São Paolo, Los Angeles, Notre Dame … the list is endless.

There is scarcely a day when I don't read or hear something from its pages, yet I had never read the whole volume before working on this book. Some parts inspire me more than anything ever written, whilst other parts bore me beyond endurance as they trace inhospitable paths through thickets of genealogies and dietary laws. Other parts depress and repel me, as sublime insights sit discordantly alongside bloodlust, arrogance and pettiness. But the Old Testament contains one of the great learning curves in literature – the story of a people's gradual, humbling discovery that God is not part of the endless cycle of violence which our human frenzy projects on to him.[11] My selection of Old Testament texts unashamedly traces a path of lights in the midst of the darkness – stars which illumine a violent night, and which, in turn, lead us to pray and work for peace.

Certain books were harder to extract from than others. The Psalms brim over with inspiring and quotable lines, whereas Job, for example, despite its glorious poetry, really needs to be read complete to make its full impact as it raises its unflinching questions about God and human suffering. Nevertheless, some of the dialogue is still extremely powerful out of context. Jewish readers might feel in general that a vital aspect is missing in any use of the Scriptures where the *story* (God working in history) is absent; and the Gospels, amongst the most condensed, compact biographical documents ever written, are extremely hard to break up. The parables in particular, Jesus' most characteristic way of teaching, make no sense unless we read them complete. I have included some extracts, but I suggest that readers return to the original text where virtually every verse of the Gospels is suitable for *lectio*. Space was the final enemy, so apologies if any readers' favourite verses are missing.

There are hundreds of English translations of the Bible, all of which try to combine accuracy with style. The New Revised Stan-

---

11. René Girard and his disciples are recommended reading for their shatteringly illuminating explorations in this and related subjects.

dard Version is used here with a few small changes for clarity or luminosity. I have arranged *The Bible as Prayer* in chronological order with numbered chapter headings in the margins as in the original, but the numbered verses have been omitted as being too cluttering and fussy for the present purpose. It should not be difficult to find the original context if desired. The deuterocanonical[12] books have been included, as most Christians in the world now and in history accept them as inspired. Anything which is God or Jesus speaking has single quotation marks; double quotation marks are used for other speech, but only if necessary for clarity. Ellipses are usually used when a repetition of some kind has been deleted, but sometimes I have taken the liberty of removing a gruesome Old Testament call for God to slaughter the writer's enemies when it is surrounded by words of great inspiration. May that same God spare me if I have offended him by so doing!

More? Reading List

There are numerous full-length books written on these subjects, but in many ways the best place to start is the Internet. Below are some random webpages to browse, although I don't necessarily agree with all of the conclusions reached by the authors.

Lectio Divina

http://www.carmelite.com/saints/other/more_5.htm
http://www.valyermo.com/ld-art.html
http://www.idahomonks.org/sect110.htm
http://www.centeringprayer.com/lectio.htm

For an Ignatian twist try the hugely popular website:

http://www.sacredspace.ie/

or the following extracts from two best-selling modern books:

---

12. The extra Old Testament books of the Hellenistic Jews, included in the Septuagint, and accepted during the period the New Testament was lived and written.

Gerard W. Hughes, *God of Surprises* (London: DLT, 1985), pp. 46–9

Anthony de Mello, *Sadhana: A Way to God, Christian Experiences in Eastern Form* (New York: Doubleday, 1978), Exercise 33

Jesus Prayer

Any Eastern Orthodox resource will have information about this most characteristic element of its spirituality. Below are two websites which give some background, and a third which suggests reading matter as well.

http://www.svots.edu/Faculty/Albert-Rossi/Articles/Saying-the-Jesus-Prayer.html

http://www.goarch.org/en/ourfaith/articles/article7104.asp

http://www.amazon.com/exec/obidos/tg/guides/guide-display/-/120GJEQ7QH2B3/104-3751687-3721521

See also Exercises 34 and 35 in Anthony de Mello, *Sadhana* (as above) for some simple ways to do vocal prayer.

Old Testament

1. HISTORY:
Words as Blood and Soil

I heard someone recently describe Christianity as a faith where feet should be firmly planted on the ground, not heads floating in the clouds. In Jewish life, too, the concrete, daily events of life are seen as the only truly authentic place in which to meet God. The daily events of the past, therefore, carefully preserved and celebrated, are a way to encounter God afresh in the present – memory itself becoming a prayer of thanksgiving for blessings received, or repentance for mistakes made. The Old Testament genealogies were reminders of those who had formed them, in flesh and in faith; and dietary laws were ways to respond constantly to God in the present by sanctifying the very food which kept them alive.

For the early Jewish people, historical events were all direct messages from God: suffering was punishment for sins; good health and long life were rewards for observance of the Law; miraculous signs proved that God was with them, and not with 'the outsiders'. Later on they began to discover that much of what was called sin actually carried within itself its own punishment – abused human freedom resulting in selfishness and rivalry, tearing apart lives, marriages and the community. In the later prophetic writings there is joy as foreigners from far-off lands are seen coming to know and love the one true God. Perhaps we can see this choice of one people, not as an exclusion of everyone else, but rather as a sign revealing that God's love is not all-encompassing in an abstract, impersonal way, but is a choice, a creative regard for every individual person who *lives and moves and has their being*[13] in Him.

---

13.   Acts 17: 28.

Genesis

1   In the beginning God created the heavens and the earth.

The breath[14] of God was moving over the face of the waters.
God said, 'Let there be light'; and there was light.

God saw everything that he had made and, indeed, it was very good.

2   God rested on the seventh day from all the work that he had done.

God formed man from the dust of the ground, and breathed into his nostrils the breath of life; and the man became a living being.

'It is not good for the man to be alone; I will make him a helper as his partner.'

9   'Be fruitful and multiply, abound on the earth and multiply in it.'

'I am establishing my covenant with you and your descendants after you.'

'I will remember my covenant that is between me and you and every living creature of all flesh.'

26   'I am the God of your father Abraham; do not be afraid, for I am with you and will bless you.'

28   'Know that I am with you and will keep you wherever you go.'

Surely the LORD is in this place – and I did not know it!

33   God has dealt graciously with me … I have everything I want.

35   God who answered me in the day of my distress and has been with me wherever I have gone.

45   Do not be distressed, or angry with yourselves.

48   God who has been my shepherd all my life to this day.

---

14.   Or spirit or wind.

Exodus

3   'I AM WHO I AM.'

14   The LORD will fight for you, and you have only to keep still.

15   'I am the LORD who heals you.'

16   In the morning you shall see the glory of the LORD.
     Draw near to the LORD.

17   'I will be standing there in front of you.'

19   'You have seen … how I bore you on eagles' wings and brought
     you to myself.'

     'Now therefore, if you obey my voice and keep my covenant, you
     shall be my treasured possession.'

20   ## The Ten Commandments[15]

     'I am the LORD your God, who brought you out of the land of
     Egypt, out of the house of slavery; you shall have no other gods
     before me.'

     'You shall not make for yourself an idol, whether in the form of
     anything that is in heaven above, or that is on the earth beneath, or
     that is in the water under the earth.'

     'You shall not make wrongful use of the name of the LORD your
     God.'

     'Remember the sabbath day, and keep it holy.'

     'Honour your father and your mother.'

     'You shall not murder.'

     'You shall not commit adultery.'

     'You shall not steal.'

---

15.   In fact, there are either nine or eleven commandments. To make ten you need either
      to combine one and two as Catholics and Lutherans do, or combine nine and ten as
      other Protestants, Orthodox and Jews do.

'You shall not bear false witness against your neighbour.'

'You shall not covet your neighbour's house.'

'You shall not covet your neighbour's wife ... or anything that belongs to your neighbour.'

22   'If your neighbour cries out to me, I will listen, for I am compassionate.'

33   The LORD used to speak to Moses face to face, as one speaks to a friend.

'My presence will go with you, and I will give you rest.'

34   'The LORD, the LORD, a God merciful and gracious, slow to anger, and abounding in steadfast love and faithfulness ... forgiving iniquity and transgression and sin.'

Leviticus

19   'You shall be holy, for I the LORD your God am holy.'

'You shall not steal; you shall not deal falsely; and you shall not lie to one another.'

'You shall not revile the deaf or put a stumbling block before the blind ... you shall not be partial to the poor or defer to the great.'

'You shall love your neighbour as yourself.'

'The alien who resides with you shall be to you as the citizen among you; you shall love the alien as yourself, for you were aliens in the land of Egypt.'

20   'You shall be holy to me; for I the LORD am holy, and I have separated you from the other peoples to be mine.'

Numbers

6   'The LORD bless you and keep you; the LORD make his face to shine upon you, and be gracious to you.'

14   The LORD is slow to anger, and abounding in steadfast love, for-
     giving iniquity and transgression.

23   God is not a human being, that he should lie, or a mortal, that he
     should change his mind. Has he promised, and will he not do it?
     Has he spoken, and will he not fulfil it?

Deuteronomy

1   In the wilderness, where you saw how the LORD your God car-
     ried you, just as one carries a child.

2   Surely the LORD your God has blessed you in all your undertakings.
     The LORD your God has been with you; you have lacked nothing.

4   You will seek the LORD your God, and you will find him if you
     search after him with all your heart and soul.

6   Hear, O Israel: The LORD is our God, the LORD alone. You shall
     love the LORD your God with all your heart, and with all your
     soul, and with all your might.

     Take care that you do not forget the LORD.

     The LORD your God you shall fear; him you shall serve, and by his
     name alone you shall swear.

7   You are a people holy to the LORD your God; the LORD your
     God has chosen you out of all the peoples on earth to be his peo-
     ple, his treasured possession.

     God will love you, bless you, and multiply you; he will bless the
     fruit of your womb and the fruit of your ground.

8   Know then in your heart that as a parent disciplines a child so the
     LORD your God disciplines you.

10   So now, O Israel, what does the LORD your God require of you?
     Only to fear the LORD your God, to walk in all his ways, to love
     him, to serve the LORD your God with all your heart and with all
     your soul.

15   If there is among you anyone in need ... do not be hard-hearted or tight-fisted toward your needy neighbour. You should rather open your hand, willingly lending enough to meet the need, whatever it may be.

Give liberally and be ungrudging when you do so, for on this account the LORD your God will bless you in all your work and in all that you undertake.

Since there will never cease to be some in need on the earth, I therefore command you: "Open your hand to the poor and needy neighbour in your land."

16   You must not distort justice; you must not show partiality.

20   Do not lose heart, or be afraid, or panic, or be in dread ... it is the LORD your God who goes with you.

30   Surely, this commandment that I am commanding you today is not too hard for you, nor is it too far away. It is not in heaven, that you should say, "Who will go up to heaven for us, and get it for us so that we may hear it and observe it?" Neither is it beyond the sea, that you should say, "Who will cross to the other side of the sea for us, and get it for us so that we may hear it and observe it?" No, the word is very near to you; it is in your mouth and in your heart for you to observe.

I have set before you life and death, blessings and curses. Choose life ... loving the LORD your God, obeying him, and holding fast to him; for that means life to you.

31   Be strong and bold; have no fear or dread of them, because it is the LORD who goes before you. He will be with you; he will not fail you or forsake you. Do not fear or be dismayed.

32   Do you thus repay the LORD, O foolish and senseless people? Is not he your father, who created you, who made you and established you?

As an eagle stirs up its nest, and hovers over its young; as it spreads its wings, takes them up, and bears them aloft on its pinions, the LORD alone guided him.

33   The beloved of the LORD rests in safety – the High God surrounds him all day long – the beloved rests between his shoulders.

Joshua

1   'I will be with you; I will not fail you or forsake you.'

'Be strong and courageous; do not be frightened or dismayed, for the LORD your God is with you wherever you go.'

The LORD your God is providing you a place of rest.

24   Now if you are unwilling to serve the LORD, choose this day whom you will serve ... but as for me and my household, we will serve the LORD

1 Samuel

2   My heart exults in the LORD; my strength is exalted in my God.

There is no Holy One like the LORD, no one besides you; there is no Rock like our God.

The LORD raises up the poor from the dust; he lifts the needy from the ash heap, to make them sit with princes and inherit a seat of honour.

3   Now the LORD came and stood there, calling as before, 'Samuel! Samuel!' And Samuel said, "Speak, for your servant is listening."

7   Direct your heart to the LORD, and serve him only.

Do not cease to cry out to the LORD our God for us, and pray that he may save us.

9   'I have seen the suffering of my people, because their outcry has come to me.'

12 Do not be afraid; you have done all this evil, yet do not turn aside from following the LORD, but serve the LORD with all your heart; and do not turn aside after useless things that cannot profit or save, for they are useless.

The LORD will not cast away his people, for his great name's sake, because it has pleased the LORD to make you a people for himself.

14 Let us draw near to God here.

16 'The LORD does not see as mortals see; they look on the outward appearance, but the LORD looks on the heart.'

25 Peace be to you, and peace be to your house, and peace be to all that you have.

2 Samuel

7 Go, do all that you have in mind; for the LORD is with you.

'I will be a father to him, and he shall be a son to me.'

You are great, O LORD God; for there is no one like you, and there is no God besides you.

22 In my distress I called upon the LORD; to my God I called. From his temple he heard my voice, and my cry came to his ears.

He reached from on high, he took me, he drew me out of mighty waters.

Indeed, you are my lamp, O LORD, the LORD lightens my darkness.

For who is God, but the LORD? And who is a rock, except our God?

24 Let us fall into the hand of the LORD, for his mercy is great.

1 Kings

3 God said [to Solomon], 'Ask what I should give you.'

I am only a little child; I do not know how to go out or come in. Give your servant therefore an understanding mind … able to discern between good and evil.

God said to him, 'Because you … have not asked for yourself long life or riches, or for the life of your enemies, but have asked for yourself understanding to discern what is right, I now do according to your word.'

'Indeed I give you a wise and discerning mind; no one like you has been before you and no one like you shall arise after you.'

19 Elijah asked that he might die: "It is enough; now, O LORD, take away my life, for I am no better than my ancestors."

The angel of the LORD came … touched Elijah, and said, "Get up and eat, otherwise the journey will be too much for you." He got up, and ate and drank; then he went in the strength of that food forty days and forty nights to Horeb the mount of God.

'Go out and stand on the mountain before the LORD, for the LORD is about to pass by.'

Now there was a great wind, so strong that it was splitting mountains and breaking rocks in pieces before the LORD, but the LORD was not in the wind.

After the wind an earthquake, but the LORD was not in the earthquake.

After the earthquake a fire, but the LORD was not in the fire.

After the fire a sound of sheer silence. When Elijah heard it, he wrapped his face in his mantle and went out and stood at the entrance of the cave.

1 Chronicles

16 Seek the LORD and his strength, seek his presence continually.

22 'Be strong and of good courage. Do not be afraid or dismayed.'

Now set your mind and heart to seek the LORD your God.

23   The LORD, the God of Israel, has given rest to his people.

28   Be strong and of good courage, and act. Do not be afraid or dis-
      mayed; for the LORD God, my God, is with you. He will not fail
      you or forsake you.

29   Yours, O LORD, are the greatness, the power, the glory, the vic-
      tory, and the majesty; for all that is in the heavens and on the earth
      is yours; yours is the kingdom, O LORD, and you are exalted as
      head above all.

      All things come from you, and of your own have we given you.

2 Chronicles

15   The LORD is with you, while you are with him. If you seek him,
      he will be found by you.

      When in their distress they turned to the LORD, the God of Israel,
      and sought him, he was found by them.

      Take courage! Do not let your hands be weak, for your work shall
      be rewarded.

16   For the eyes of the LORD range throughout the entire earth, to
      strengthen those whose heart is true to him.

20   We do not know what to do, but our eyes are on you, [O LORD].

30   The LORD your God is gracious and merciful, and will not turn
      away his face from you, if you return to him.

Nehemiah

1   O LORD God of heaven, the great and awesome God who keeps
      covenant and steadfast love with those who love him and keep his
      commandments; let your ear be attentive and your eyes open to

hear the prayer of your servant that I now pray before you day and night.

8   The joy of the LORD is your strength.

9   You are the LORD, you alone; you have made heaven, the heaven of heavens, with all their host, the earth and all that is on it, the seas and all that is in them. To all of them you give life, and the host of heaven worships you.

Tobit

4   Revere the Lord all your days, my son, and refuse to sin or to transgress his commandments. Live uprightly all the days of your life, and do not walk in the ways of wrongdoing; for those who act in accordance with truth will prosper in all their activities.

Do not turn your face away from anyone who is poor, and the face of God will not be turned away from you.

If you have many possessions, make your gift from them in proportion; if few, do not be afraid to give according to the little you have. So you will be laying up a good treasure for yourself against the day of necessity. For almsgiving delivers from death and keeps you from going into the Darkness.

Do not drink wine to excess or let drunkenness go with you on your way. Give some of your food to the hungry, and some of your clothing to the naked. Give all your surplus as alms, and do not let your eye begrudge your giving of alms.

[Tobit said] Do not be afraid, my son, because we have become poor. You have great wealth if you fear God and flee from every sin and do what is good in the sight of the Lord your God.

5   Take courage; the time is near for God to heal you; take courage.

12   Prayer with fasting is good, but better than both is almsgiving with righteousness.

It is better to give alms than to lay up gold. For almsgiving saves from death and purges away every sin. Those who give alms will enjoy a full life, but those who commit sin and do wrong are their own worst enemies.

Judith

8   You cannot plumb the depths of the human heart or understand the workings of the human mind; how do you expect to search out God, who made all these things, and find out his mind or comprehend his thought?

Do not try to bind the purposes of the Lord our God; for God is not like a human being, to be threatened, or like a mere mortal, to be won over by pleading.

9   Your strength [O God] does not depend on numbers, nor your might on the powerful. But you are the God of the lowly, helper of the oppressed, upholder of the weak, protector of the forsaken, saviour of those without hope.

2. POETRY:
Words as Song and Prayer

Poetry and prayer are siblings. Both aim to rise above the everyday use of words and images in a search for transcendence – words to go beyond words. In this section of the book we see writers soaring to the heights and sinking to the depths of the human experience. What is particularly striking is the complete honesty of the emotions conveyed. There is no attempt to disguise or to cover up doubts or despair; and there is a willingness, free from all human respect or propriety, to be seen dancing and shouting for joy. Indeed, the writers' carefree ability to allow their hearts such emotional outpouring is a striking example of spiritual (and mental) health, and is almost modern in its instinctive understanding of psychology. When Jesus told his disciples to go to their rooms, shut the door and pray in secret,[16] it was surely to enable them to be similarly honest before God, and free from any concern about what others might think, whether good or bad. In this section too are the wisdom writings, collections of pithy sayings which combine common sense and spiritual elevation in poetic form. Their moderation and warmth is a far cry from Puritanism and celebrates the blessings of human life with reverence and with a twinkle of the eye.

Job

1   Job was blameless and upright, one who feared God and turned away from evil.

Then Satan answered the LORD, "Does Job fear God for nothing? ... But stretch out your hand now, and touch all that he has, and he will curse you to your face."

---

16.   Matt. 6: 6.

Naked I came from my mother's womb, and naked shall I return there; the LORD gave, and the LORD has taken away; blessed be the name of the LORD.

2   Satan inflicted loathsome sores on Job from the sole of his foot to the crown of his head ... His wife said to him, "Do you still persist in your integrity? Curse God, and die." But he said to her, "You speak as any foolish woman would speak. Shall we receive the good at the hand of God, and not receive the bad?"

3   Job said: "Let the day perish in which I was born ... let that day be darkness! ... let no joyful cry be heard in it ... let it hope for light, but have none ... because it did not shut the doors of my mother's womb, and hide trouble from my eyes."

Why did I not die at birth, come forth from the womb and expire? ... Now I would be lying down and quiet; I would be asleep; then I would be at rest.

Why is light given to one in misery, and life to the bitter in soul, who long for death, but it does not come, and dig for it more than for hidden treasures?

Truly the thing that I fear comes upon me, and what I dread befalls me.

I am not at ease, nor am I quiet; I have no rest; but trouble comes.

4   See, [Job], you have instructed many; you have strengthened the weak hands. Your words have supported those who were stumbling, and you have made firm the feeble knees. But now it has come to you, and you are impatient; it touches you, and you are dismayed.

5   Human beings are born to trouble just as sparks fly upward.

I would seek God, and to God I would commit my cause. He does great things and unsearchable, marvellous things without number.

He gives rain on the earth and sends waters on the fields; he sets on high those who are lowly, and those who mourn are lifted to safety.

How happy is the one whom God reproves; therefore do not despise the discipline of the Almighty. For he wounds, but he binds up; he strikes, but his hands heal.

At destruction and famine you shall laugh, and shall not fear the wild animals of the earth. For you shall be in league with the stones of the field, and the wild animals shall be at peace with you.

6   O that my vexation were weighed, and all my calamity laid in the balances! For then it would be heavier than the sand of the sea.

What is my strength, that I should wait? And what is my end, that I should be patient? Is my strength the strength of stones, or is my flesh bronze? In truth I have no help in me, and any resource is driven from me.

7   Do not human beings have a hard service on earth, and are not their days like the days of a labourer?

When I lie down I say: When shall I rise? But the night is long, and I am full of tossing until dawn.

My days are swifter than a weaver's shuttle, and come to their end without hope.

Therefore I will not restrain my mouth; I will speak in the anguish of my spirit; I will complain in the bitterness of my soul.

I loathe my life; I would not live forever. Let me alone, for my days are a breath.

What are human beings, that you make so much of them, that you set your mind on them, visit them every morning, test them every moment?

If I sin, what do I do to you, you watcher of humanity? Why have you made me your target? Why have I become a burden to you? Why do you not pardon my transgression and take away my iniquity?

8   We know nothing, for our days on earth are but a shadow.

9   How can a mortal be just before God? If one wished to contend

with him, one could not answer him once in a thousand. He is wise in heart, and mighty in strength – who has resisted him, and succeeded?

God will not let me get my breath, but fills me with bitterness. If it is a contest of strength, he is the strong one! If it is a matter of justice, who can summon him?

God is not a mortal, as I am, that I might answer him, that we should come to trial together. There is no umpire between us, who might lay his hand on us both.

10   I loathe my life; I will give free utterance to my complaint; I will speak in the bitterness of my soul. I will say to God, Do not condemn me; let me know why you contend against me. Does it seem good to you God to oppress, to despise the work of your hands and favour the schemes of the wicked?

Your hands fashioned and made me; and now you turn and destroy me. Remember that you fashioned me like clay; and will you turn me to dust again?

11   Can you find out the deep things of God? Can you find out the limit of the Almighty? It is higher than heaven – what can you do? Deeper than Sheol – what can you know? Its measure is longer than the earth, and broader than the sea.

12   In God's hand is the life of every living thing and the breath of every human being.

15   Are the consolations of God too small for you, or the word that deals gently with you? Why does your heart carry you away, and why do your eyes flash, so that you turn your spirit against God, and let such words go out of your mouth?

What are mortals, that they can be clean? Or those born of woman, that they can be righteous?

19   I know that my Redeemer lives, and that at the last he will stand

upon the earth; and after my skin has been thus destroyed, then in my flesh I shall see God.

23 Oh, that I knew where I might find God, that I might come even to his dwelling! I would lay my case before him, and fill my mouth with arguments. I would learn what he would answer me, and understand what he would say to me.

God knows the way that I take; when he has tested me, I shall come out like gold. My foot has held fast to his steps; I have kept his way and have not turned aside.

God stands alone and who can dissuade him? What he desires, that he does. Therefore I am terrified at his presence; when I consider, I am in dread of him ... If only I could vanish in darkness, and thick darkness would cover my face!

24 From the city the dying groan, and the throat of the wounded cries for help; yet God pays no attention to their prayer.

27 As God lives, who has taken away my right, and the Almighty, who has made my soul bitter, as long as my breath is in me and the spirit of God is in my nostrils, my lips will not speak falsehood, and my tongue will not utter deceit.

28 Where shall wisdom be found? And where is the place of understanding? Mortals do not know the way to it, and it is not found in the land of the living.

Truly, the fear of the Lord, that is wisdom; and to depart from evil is understanding.

29 Oh, that I were as in the months of old, as in the days when God watched over me; when his lamp shone over my head, and by his light I walked through darkness.

I was eyes to the blind, and feet to the lame. I was a father to the needy, and I championed the cause of the stranger.

30 My soul is poured out within me; days of affliction have taken hold

of me. The night racks my bones, and the pain that gnaws me takes no rest.

I cry to you [O God] and you do not answer me; I stand, and you merely look at me.

Surely one does not turn against the needy, when in disaster they cry for help. Did I not weep for those whose day was hard? Was not my soul grieved for the poor? But when I looked for good, evil came; and when I waited for light, darkness came.

33   The spirit of God has made me, and the breath of the Almighty gives me life.

34   If God should take back his spirit to himself, and gather to himself his breath, all flesh would perish together, and all mortals return to dust.

38   The LORD answered Job out of the whirlwind: 'Where were you when I laid the foundation of the earth?'

Psalms

1   Happy is the one who does not follow the advice of the wicked ... but whose delight is the law of the LORD, and on his law meditates day and night.

Such a one is like a tree planted by streams of water, yielding its fruit in due season, leaves never withering.

4   Answer me when I call, O God of my right! You gave me room when I was in distress. Be gracious to me, and hear my prayer.

The LORD hears when I call to him.

When you are disturbed, do not sin; ponder it on your beds, and be silent ... and put your trust in the LORD.

Let the light of your face shine on us, O LORD!

I will both lie down and sleep in peace; for you alone, O LORD, make me lie down in safety.

5   O LORD, in the morning you hear my voice.

Let all who take refuge in you rejoice; let them ever sing for joy. Spread your protection over them, so that those who love your name may exult in you.

6   Be gracious to me, O LORD, for I am languishing; O LORD, heal me, for my bones are shaking with terror. My soul also is struck with terror … O LORD – how long?

Turn, O LORD, save my life; deliver me for the sake of your steadfast love.

I am weary with my moaning; every night I flood my bed with tears; I drench my couch with my weeping.

The LORD has heard the sound of my weeping. The LORD has heard my supplication; the LORD accepts my prayer.

7   O LORD my God, in you I take refuge.

8   O LORD, our Sovereign, how majestic is your name in all the earth! You have set your glory above the heavens.

When I look at your heavens, the work of your fingers, the moon and the stars that you have established, what are human beings that you are mindful of them, mortals that you care for them?

Yet you have made them a little lower than the angels, and crowned them with glory and honour; you have given them dominion over the works of your hands; you have put all things under their feet.

9   I will give thanks to the LORD with my whole heart; I will tell of all your wonderful deeds.

I will be glad and exult in you; I will sing praise to your name, O Most High.

The LORD is a stronghold for the oppressed, a stronghold in times of trouble.

Those who know your name put their trust in you; for you, O LORD, have not forsaken those who seek you.

10   Why, O LORD, do you stand far off? Why do you hide yourself in times of trouble?

Rise up, O LORD; O God, lift up your hand; do not forget the oppressed.

O LORD, you will hear the desire of the meek; you will strengthen their heart, you will incline your ear to do justice for the orphan and the oppressed.

13   How long, O LORD? Will you forget me forever? How long will you hide your face from me? How long must I bear pain in my soul, and have sorrow in my heart all day long?

I trusted in your steadfast love; my heart shall rejoice in your salvation.

I will sing to the LORD, because he has dealt bountifully with me.

15   O LORD, who may abide in your tent? Who may dwell on your holy hill? The one who walks blamelessly, and does what is right, and speaks the truth from his heart.

16   Protect me, O God, for in you I take refuge. I say to the LORD: You are my Lord; I have no good apart from you.

I bless the LORD who gives me counsel; in the night too my heart instructs me.

I keep the LORD always before me; because he is at my right hand, I shall not be moved.

Therefore my heart is glad, and my soul rejoices; my body also rests secure.

You show me the path of life. In your presence there is fulness of joy; in your right hand are pleasures forevermore.

17   I call upon you, for you will answer me, O God; incline your ear to me, hear my words.

Guard me as the apple of the eye; hide me in the shadow of your wings.

18   I love you, O LORD, my strength.

       The LORD is my rock, my fortress, and my deliverer, my God, my rock in whom I take refuge, my shield, and the horn of my salvation, my stronghold.

       In my distress I called upon the LORD; to my God I cried for help. From his temple he heard my voice, and my cry to him reached his ears.

       He reached down from on high, he took me; he drew me out of mighty waters ... The LORD was my support.

       He brought me out into a broad place; he delivered me, because he delighted in me.

       It is you who light my lamp; the LORD, my God, lights up my darkness.

19   The heavens are telling the glory of God; and the firmament proclaims his handiwork.

       Let the words of my mouth and the meditation of my heart be acceptable to you, O LORD, my rock and my redeemer.

20   The LORD answer you in the day of trouble! ... May he grant you your heart's desire, and fulfil all your plans.

22   My God, my God, why have you forsaken me? Why are you so far from helping me, from the words of my groaning?

       O my God, I cry by day, but you do not answer; and by night, but find no rest.

       Yet it was you who took me from the womb; you kept me safe on my mother's breast. On you I was cast from my birth, and since my mother bore me you have been my God.

       Do not be far from me, for trouble is near and there is no one to help.

       I am poured out like water, and all my bones are out of joint; my heart is like wax; it is melted within my breast.

O LORD, do not be far away! O my help, come quickly to my aid!

All the ends of the earth shall remember and turn to the LORD; and all the families of the nations shall worship before him.

23 The LORD is my shepherd, I shall not want.

He makes me lie down in green pastures; he leads me beside still waters; he restores my soul.

Even though I walk through the darkest valley, I fear no evil; for you are with me; your rod and your staff – they comfort me.

Surely goodness and mercy shall follow me all the days of my life, and I shall dwell in the house of the LORD my whole life long.

24 The earth is the Lord's and all that is in it, the world, and those who live in it.

Who shall ascend the hill of the LORD? And who shall stand in his holy place? The one who has clean hands and a pure heart, who does not lift up his soul to what is false.

25 To you, O LORD, I lift up my soul. O my God, in you I trust.

Make me to know your ways, O LORD; teach me your paths.

Lead me in your truth, and teach me, for you are the God of my salvation; for you I wait all day long.

God leads the humble in what is right, and teaches them his way.

For your name's sake, O LORD, pardon my guilt, for it is great.

My eyes are ever toward the LORD, for he will pluck my feet out of the net.

Turn to me and be gracious to me, for I am lonely and afflicted.

Relieve the troubles of my heart, and bring me out of my distress.

Consider my affliction and my trouble, and forgive all my sins.

O guard my life, and deliver me; do not let me be put to shame, for I take refuge in you.

27 The LORD is my light and my salvation; whom shall I fear? The LORD is the stronghold of my life; of whom shall I be afraid?

Though an army encamp against me, my heart shall not fear; though war rise up against me, yet I will be confident.

One thing I asked of the LORD, that will I seek after: to live in the house of the LORD all the days of my life.

The LORD will hide me in his shelter in the day of trouble; he will conceal me under the cover of his tent; he will set me high on a rock.

Hear, O LORD, when I cry aloud, be gracious to me and answer me!

Your face, LORD, do I seek.

Do not hide your face from me ... Do not cast me off, do not forsake me, O God of my salvation!

If my father and mother forsake me, the LORD will take me up.

I believe that I shall see the goodness of the LORD in the land of the living.

Wait for the LORD; be strong, and let your heart take courage; wait for the LORD!

28 To you, O LORD, I call; my rock, do not refuse to hear me. Hear the voice of my supplication, as I cry to you for help.

Blessed be the LORD, for he has heard the sound of my pleadings.

The LORD is my strength and my shield; in him my heart trusts; so I am helped, and my heart exults, and with my song I give thanks to him.

30 O LORD my God, I cried to you for help, and you have healed me. Weeping may linger for the night, but joy comes with the morning.

Hear, O LORD, and be gracious to me! O LORD, be my helper!

You have turned my mourning into dancing; you have taken off my sackcloth and clothed me with joy, so that my soul may praise you and not be silent. O LORD my God, I will give thanks to you forever.

31 In you, O LORD, I seek refuge; do not let me ever be put to shame; in your righteousness deliver me.

Incline your ear to me; rescue me speedily. Be a rock of refuge for me, a strong fortress to save me.

Into your hand I commit my spirit; you have redeemed me, O LORD, faithful God.

Be gracious to me, O LORD, for I am in distress.

I trust in you, O LORD; I say: You are my God.

My times are in your hand ... Let your face shine upon your servant; save me in your steadfast love.

O how abundant is your goodness that you have laid up for those who fear you, and accomplished for those who take refuge in you.

Be strong, and let your heart take courage, all you who wait for the LORD.

32 Happy are those whose transgression is forgiven, whose sin is covered.

I acknowledged my sin to you, and I did not hide my iniquity, and you forgave the guilt of my sin.

Let all who are faithful offer prayer to you; at a time of distress, the rush of mighty waters shall not reach them.

You are a hiding place for me; you preserve me from trouble; you surround me with glad cries of deliverance.

Many are the torments of the wicked, but steadfast love surrounds those who trust in the LORD.

33 The earth is full of the steadfast love of the LORD.

Let all the earth fear the LORD; let all the inhabitants of the world stand in awe of him. For he spoke, and it came to be; he commanded, and it stood firm.

The LORD looks down from heaven; he sees all humankind ... he who fashions the hearts of them all, and observes all their deeds.

Truly the eye of the LORD is on those who fear him, on those who hope in his steadfast love, to deliver their soul from death, and to keep them alive in famine.

Our soul waits for the LORD; he is our help and shield.

Our heart is glad in him, because we trust in his holy name.

Let your steadfast love, O LORD, be upon us, as we place all our hope in you.

34   I will bless the LORD at all times; his praise shall continually be in my mouth.

I sought the LORD, and he answered me, and delivered me from all my fears.

Look to him, and be radiant; so your faces shall never be ashamed.

This poor soul cried, and was heard by the LORD, and was saved from every trouble.

The angel of the LORD encamps around those who fear him, and delivers them.

O taste and see that the LORD is good; happy are those who take refuge in him.

The eyes of the LORD are on the righteous, and his ears are open to their cry; when [they] cry for help, the LORD hears, and rescues them from all their troubles.

The LORD is near to the brokenhearted, and saves the crushed in spirit.

The LORD redeems the life of his servants; none of those who take refuge in him will be condemned.

36   Your steadfast love, O LORD, extends to the heavens, your faithfulness to the clouds.

How precious is your steadfast love, O God! All people may take refuge in the shadow of your wings.

With you [O LORD] is the fountain of life; in your light we see light.

37 Take delight in the LORD, and he will give you the desires of your heart.

Commit your way to the LORD; trust in him, and he will act.

Be still before the LORD, and wait patiently for him.

Refrain from anger, and forsake wrath. Do not fret – it leads only to evil.

The meek shall inherit the land, and delight in abundant prosperity.

Our steps are made firm by the LORD, when he delights in our way; though we stumble, we shall not fall headlong, for the LORD holds us by the hand.

The LORD loves justice; he will not forsake his faithful ones. The righteous shall be kept safe forever.

38 I am utterly bowed down and prostrate; all day long I go around mourning.

I am utterly spent and crushed; I groan because of the tumult of my heart.

O Lord, all my longing is known to you; my sighing is not hidden from you.

My heart throbs, my strength fails me; as for the light of my eyes – it also has gone from me.

But it is for you, O LORD, that I wait; it is you, O LORD my God, who will answer.

Do not forsake me, O LORD; O my God, do not be far from me; make haste to help me, O Lord, my salvation.

39 LORD, let me know my end, and what is the measure of my days; let me know how fleeting my life is.

You have made my days a mere handbreadth, and my lifetime is as nothing in your sight.

Hear my prayer, O LORD, and give ear to my cry; do not hold your peace at my tears. For I am your passing guest, an alien, like all my forebears.

40   I waited patiently for the LORD; he inclined to me and heard my cry.

He drew me up from the desolate pit, out of the miry bog, and set my feet upon a rock, making my steps secure.

He put a new song in my mouth, a song of praise to our God.

Happy are those who make the LORD their trust.

Here I am. I delight to do your will, O my God; your law is within my heart.

I have not hidden your saving help within my heart, I have spoken of your faithfulness and your salvation.

Do not, O LORD, withhold your mercy from me; let your steadfast love and your faithfulness keep me safe forever.

Be pleased, O LORD, to deliver me; O LORD, make haste to help me.

May all who seek you rejoice and be glad in you; may those who love your salvation say continually: Great is the LORD!

41   Happy are those who consider the poor; the LORD delivers them in the day of trouble.

The LORD sustains them on their sickbed; in their illness you heal all their infirmities.

42   As a deer longs for flowing streams, so my soul longs for you, O God.

My soul thirsts for God, for the living God. When shall I come and behold the face of God?

Why are you cast down, O my soul, and why are you disquieted within me? Hope in God; I shall praise him again, my help and my God.

By day the LORD commands his steadfast love, and at night his song is with me, a prayer to the God of my life.

43 You are the God in whom I take refuge; why have you cast me off? O send out your light and your truth; let them be my guide.

44 Rouse yourself! Why do you sleep, O Lord? Awake, do not cast us off forever!

Why do you hide your face? Why do you forget our affliction and oppression?

46 God is our refuge and strength, a very present help in trouble.

We will not fear, though the earth should change, though the mountains shake in the heart of the sea; though its waters roar and foam, though the mountains tremble with its tumult.

'Be still, and know that I am God.'

51 Have mercy on me, O God, according to your steadfast love; according to your abundant mercy blot out my transgressions.

Wash me thoroughly from my iniquity, and cleanse me from my sin.

I know my transgressions, and my sin is ever before me. Against you alone [O Lord] have I sinned, and done what is evil in your sight.

You are justified in your sentence and blameless when you pass judgment. Indeed, I was born guilty, a sinner when my mother conceived me.

You desire truth in the inward being; therefore teach me wisdom in my secret heart.

Purge me with hyssop, and I shall be clean; wash me, and I shall be whiter than snow.

Let me hear joy and gladness; let the bones that you have crushed rejoice.

Hide your face from my sins, and blot out all my iniquities.

Create in me a clean heart, O God, and put a new and right spirit within me.

Do not cast me away from your presence, and do not take your holy spirit from me.

Restore to me the joy of your salvation, and sustain in me a willing spirit.

Then I will teach transgressors your ways, and sinners will return to you.

O Lord, open my lips, and my mouth will declare your praise.

You have no delight in sacrifice; if I were to give a burnt offering, you would not be pleased. The sacrifice acceptable to God is a broken spirit; a broken and contrite heart, O God, you will not despise.

54   God is my helper; the Lord is the upholder of my life.

55   Give ear to my prayer, O God; do not hide yourself from my supplication. Attend to me, and answer me; I am troubled in my complaint.

My heart is in anguish within me, the terrors of death have fallen upon me.

Fear and trembling come upon me, and horror overwhelms me.

O that I had wings like a dove! I would fly away and be at rest; truly, I would flee far away; I would lodge in the wilderness.

Cast your burden on the LORD, and he will sustain you.

56   In God I trust; I am not afraid. What can a mere mortal do to me?

You have delivered my soul from death, and my feet from stumbling, so that I may walk before God in the light of life.

57   Be merciful to me, O God, be merciful to me, for in you my soul takes refuge; in the shadow of your wings I will take refuge, until the destroying storms pass by.

God will send forth his steadfast love and his faithfulness.

Awake, my soul! Awake, O harp and lyre! I will awake the dawn.

Your steadfast love is as high as the heavens; your faithfulness extends to the clouds.

62   My soul finds rest in God alone.

For God alone my soul waits in silence.

God alone is my rock and my salvation, my fortress; I shall never be shaken.

Trust in God at all times, O people; pour out your heart before him.

63   O God, you are my God, I seek you, my soul thirsts for you; my flesh faints for you, as in a dry and weary land where there is no water.

Your steadfast love is better than life, my lips will praise you.

I will bless you as long as I live; I will lift up my hands and call on your name.

I think of you on my bed, and meditate on you in the watches of the night; for you have been my help.

In the shadow of your wings I sing for joy.

My soul clings to you; your right hand upholds me.

66   Make a joyful noise to God, all the earth.

Truly God has listened; he has given heed to the words of my prayer.

Blessed be God, because he has not rejected my prayer or removed his steadfast love from me.

67   May God be gracious to us and bless us and make his face to shine upon us.

69   Save me, O God, for the waters have come up to my neck. I sink in deep mire, where there is no foothold; I have come into deep waters, and the flood sweeps over me.

I am weary with my crying; my throat is parched. My eyes grow dim with waiting for my God.

O God, you know my folly; the wrongs I have done are not hidden from you.

Do not let those who hope in you be put to shame because of me, O Lord GOD of hosts.

My prayer is to you, O LORD. At an acceptable time, O God, in the abundance of your steadfast love, answer me.

Do not let the flood sweep over me, or the deep swallow me up, or the Pit close its mouth over me.

Answer me, O LORD, for your steadfast love is good; according to your abundant mercy, turn to me.

Do not hide your face from your servant, for I am in distress – make haste to answer me.

I am in despair. I looked for pity, but there was none; and for comforters, but I found none.

The LORD hears the needy, and does not despise his own that are in bonds.

71 You, O Lord, are my hope, my trust, O LORD, from my youth.

Upon you [O LORD] I have leaned from my birth; it was you who took me from my mother's womb.

Do not cast me off in the time of old age [O LORD]; do not forsake me when my strength is spent.

O God, do not be far from me; O my God, make haste to help me!

O God, from my youth you have taught me, and I still proclaim your wondrous deeds.

Even to old age and gray hairs, O God, do not forsake me.

73 Whom have I in heaven but you [O God]? And there is nothing on earth that I desire other than you.

My flesh and my heart may fail, but God is the strength of my heart and my portion forever.

It is good to be near God.

77   In the day of my trouble I seek the Lord; in the night my hand is stretched out without wearying; my soul refuses to be comforted.

      I think of God, and I moan; I meditate, and my spirit faints. You keep my eyelids from closing; I am so troubled that I cannot speak.

      I commune with my heart in the night; I meditate and search my spirit.

84   Happy are those whose strength is in you.

      A day in your courts is better than a thousand elsewhere. I would rather be a doorkeeper in the house of my God than live in the tents of wickedness.

      O LORD of hosts, happy is everyone who trusts in you.

85   Show us your steadfast love, O LORD, and grant us your salvation.

      Let me hear what God the LORD will speak, for he will speak peace to his people, to his faithful, to those who turn to him in their hearts.

      Steadfast love and faithfulness will meet; righteousness and peace will kiss.

86   Incline your ear, O LORD, and answer me, for I am poor and needy.

      Preserve my life, for I am devoted to you; save your servant who trusts in you.

      You are my God; be gracious to me, O Lord, for to you do I cry all day long.

      Gladden the soul of your servant, for to you, O Lord, I lift up my soul.

      You, O Lord, are good and forgiving, abounding in steadfast love to all who call on you.

      Give ear, O LORD, to my prayer; listen to my cry of supplication.

      In the day of my trouble I call on you, for you will answer me.

Teach me your way, O LORD, that I may walk in your truth; give me an undivided heart to revere your name.

You, O Lord, are a God merciful and gracious, slow to anger and abounding in steadfast love and faithfulness.

88 O LORD, God of my salvation, when, at night, I cry out in your presence, let my prayer come before you; incline your ear to my cry.

Every day I call on you, O LORD; I spread out my hands to you.

I, O LORD, cry out to you; in the morning my prayer comes before you.

O LORD, why do you cast me off? Why do you hide your face from me? Wretched and close to death from my youth up, I suffer your terrors; I am desperate.

90 Lord, you have been our refuge in every generation.

Before the mountains were brought forth, or ever you had formed the earth and the world, from everlasting to everlasting you are God.

A thousand years in your sight are like yesterday when it is past, or like a watch in the night.

The days of our life are seventy years, or perhaps eighty, if we are strong; even then their span is only toil and trouble; they are soon gone, and we fly away.

Teach us to count our days that we may gain wisdom of heart.

Turn, O LORD! How long? Have compassion on your servants!

Satisfy us in the morning with your steadfast love, so that we may rejoice and be glad all our days.

Let the favour of the Lord our God be upon us, and prosper for us the work of our hands.

91 You who live in the shelter of the Most High, who abide in the

shadow of the Almighty, will say to the LORD: My refuge and my fortress; my God, in whom I trust.

You will not fear the terror of the night, or the arrow that flies by day, or the pestilence that stalks in darkness, or the destruction that wastes at noonday.

You have made the LORD your refuge, the Most High your dwelling place.

He will command his angels concerning you to guard you in all your ways. On their hands they will bear you up, so that you will not dash your foot against a stone.

'Those who love me, I will deliver; I will protect those who know my name. When they call to me, I will answer them; I will be with them in trouble, I will rescue them and honour them.'

92 It is good to give thanks to the LORD ... to declare your steadfast love in the morning, and your faithfulness by night.

95 O come, let us sing to the LORD; let us make a joyful noise to the rock of our salvation!

Let us come into God's presence with thanksgiving; let us make a joyful noise to him with songs of praise!

In God's hand are the depths of the earth; the heights of the mountains are his also.

O come, let us worship and bow down, let us kneel before the LORD, our Maker! For he is our God, and we are the people of his pasture, and the sheep of his hand.

96 O sing to the LORD a new song; sing to the LORD, all the earth ... tell of his salvation from day to day.

Let the heavens be glad, and let the earth rejoice; let the sea roar, and all that fills it; let the field exult, and everything in it.

98 Make a joyful noise to the LORD, all the earth; break forth into joyous song and sing praises.

Let the floods clap their hands; let the hills sing together for joy at the presence of the LORD, for he is coming to judge the earth. He will judge the world with righteousness, and the peoples with equity.

100 Worship the LORD with gladness; come into his presence with singing.

Know that the LORD is God. It is he that made us, and we are his; we are his people, and the sheep of his pasture.

Enter his gates with thanksgiving, and his courts with praise. Give thanks to him, bless his name.

The LORD is good; his steadfast love endures forever, and his faithfulness to all generations.

102 Hear my prayer, O LORD; let my cry come to you.

Do not hide your face from me in the day of my distress. Incline your ear to me; answer me speedily in the day when I call.

103 Bless the LORD, O my soul, and all that is within me, bless his holy name.

Bless the LORD, O my soul, and do not forget all his benefits – who forgives all your iniquity, who heals all your diseases, who redeems your life from the Pit, who crowns you with steadfast love and mercy.

The LORD is merciful and gracious, slow to anger and abounding in steadfast love.

He does not deal with us according to our sins, nor repay us according to our iniquities.

As the heavens are high above the earth, so great is God's steadfast love toward those who fear him.

As far as the east is from the west, so far he removes our transgressions from us.

As a father has compassion for his children, so the LORD has compassion for those who fear him. For he knows how we were made; he remembers that we are dust.

The steadfast love of the LORD is from everlasting to everlasting on those who fear him.

104 O LORD my God, you are very great. You are clothed with honour and majesty, wrapped in light as with a garment.

You make springs gush forth in the valleys; they flow between the hills, giving drink to every wild animal. By the streams the birds of the air have their habitation; they sing among the branches.

The earth is full of your creatures. When you hide your face, they are dismayed; when you take away their breath, they die and return to their dust. When you send forth your spirit, they are created; and you renew the face of the earth.

I will sing to the LORD as long as I live; I will sing praise to my God while I have being.

105 O give thanks to the LORD, call on his name, make known his deeds among the peoples. Sing to him, sing praises to him; tell of all his wonderful works.

Glory in his holy name; let the hearts of those who seek the LORD rejoice.

Seek the LORD and his strength; seek his presence continually.

108 My heart is steadfast, O God, my heart is steadfast; I will sing and make melody. Awake, my soul! Awake, O harp and lyre! I will awake the dawn.

112 Praise the LORD! Happy are those who fear the LORD, who greatly delight in his commandments.

They rise in the darkness as a light for the upright; they are gracious, merciful, and righteous.

It is well with those who deal generously and lend, who conduct their affairs with justice.

[The righteous] are not afraid of evil tidings; their hearts are firm, secure in the LORD. Their hearts are steady, they will not be afraid.

113 The LORD raises the poor from the dust, and lifts the needy from the ash heap, to make them sit with princes, with the princes of his people.

115 Not to us, O LORD, not to us, but to your name give glory, for the sake of your steadfast love and your faithfulness.

116 I love the LORD, because he has heard my voice and my supplications. Because he inclined his ear to me, therefore I will call on him as long as I live.

The snares of death encompassed me; the pangs of Sheol laid hold on me; I suffered distress and anguish. Then I called on the name of the LORD: O LORD, save my life!

Gracious is the LORD, and righteous; our God is merciful.

The LORD protects the simple; when I was brought low, he saved me.

Return, O my soul, to your rest, for the LORD has dealt bountifully with you.

You have delivered my soul from death, my eyes from tears, my feet from stumbling.

I walk before the LORD in the land of the living.

What shall I return to the LORD for all his bounty to me? I will lift up the cup of salvation and call on the name of the LORD.

Precious in the sight of the LORD is the death of his faithful ones.

118 O give thanks to the LORD, for he is good; his steadfast love endures forever!

Out of my distress I called on the LORD; the LORD answered me and set me in a broad place.

With the LORD on my side I do not fear. What can mortals do to me?

It is better to take refuge in the LORD than to put confidence in mortals.

I was pushed hard, so that I was falling, but the LORD helped me.

The LORD is my strength and my might; he has become my salvation.

The stone that the builders rejected has become the chief cornerstone. This is the Lord's doing; it is marvellous in our eyes.

This is the day that the LORD has made; let us rejoice and be glad in it.

Blessed is the one who comes in the name of the LORD.

119 Happy are those whose way is blameless, who walk in the law of the LORD.

With my whole heart I seek you; do not let me stray from your commandments.

I treasure your word in my heart, so that I may not sin against you.

I delight in the way of your decrees as much as in all riches.

I will meditate on your precepts, and fix my eyes on your ways.

I will delight in your statutes; I will not forget your word.

Open my eyes, so that I may behold wondrous things out of your law.

My soul is consumed with longing for your ordinances at all times.

Your decrees are my delight, they are my counsellors.

Make me understand the way of your precepts, and I will meditate on your wondrous works.

My soul melts away for sorrow; strengthen me according to your word.

Put false ways far from me; and graciously teach me your law.

Give me understanding, that I may keep your law and observe it with my whole heart.

Turn my eyes from looking at vanities; give me life in your ways.

I will keep your law continually, forever and ever.

I shall walk at liberty, for I have sought your precepts.

I will also speak of your decrees before kings, and shall not be put to shame.

I find my delight in your commandments, because I love them.

This is my comfort in my distress, that your promise gives me life.

Your statutes have been my songs wherever I make my home.

I remember your name in the night, O LORD, and keep your law.

The earth, O LORD, is full of your steadfast love; teach me your statutes.

Teach me good judgment and knowledge, for I believe in your commandments.

Before I was humbled I went astray, but now I keep your word.

The law of your mouth is better to me than thousands of gold and silver pieces.

Your hands have made and fashioned me; give me understanding that I may learn your commandments.

Let your mercy come to me, that I may live; for your law is my delight.

My soul languishes for your salvation; I hope in your word.

The LORD exists forever; your word is firmly fixed in heaven.

If your law had not been my delight, I would have perished in my misery.

I will never forget your precepts, for by them you have given me life.

I am yours; save me, for I have sought your precepts.

Oh, how I love your law! It is my meditation all day long.

I have more understanding than all my teachers, for your decrees are my meditation.

I understand more than the aged, for I keep your precepts.

I hold back my feet from every evil way, in order to keep your word.

How sweet are your words to my taste, sweeter than honey to my mouth!

Your word is a lamp to my feet and a light to my path.

You are my hiding place and my shield; I hope in your word.

The unfolding of your words gives light; it imparts understanding to the simple.

Make your face shine upon your servant, and teach me your statutes.

My eyes shed streams of tears because your law is not kept.

Trouble and anguish have come upon me, but your commandments are my delight.

I rise before dawn and cry for help; I put my hope in your words.

You are near, O LORD, and all your commandments are true.

I rejoice at your word like one who finds great spoil.

Great peace have those who love your law; nothing can make them stumble.

I keep your precepts and decrees, for all my ways are before you.

Let my cry come before you, O LORD; give me understanding according to your word.

I long for your salvation, O LORD, and your law is my delight.

I have gone astray like a lost sheep; seek out your servant, for I do not forget your commandments.

121 I lift up my eyes to the hills – from where will my help come? My help comes from the LORD, who made heaven and earth.

The LORD will keep your going out and your coming in from this time on and forevermore.

123 As the eyes of servants look to the hand of their master, as the eyes

of a maid to the hand of her mistress, so our eyes look to the LORD our God, until he has mercy upon us.

124 We have escaped like a bird from the snare of the fowlers; the snare is broken, and we have escaped. Our help is in the name of the LORD, who made heaven and earth.

126 May those who sow in tears reap with shouts of joy. Those who go out weeping, bearing the seed for sowing, shall come home with shouts of joy, carrying their sheaves.

127 Unless the LORD builds the house, those who build it labour in vain. Unless the LORD guards the city, the guard keeps watch in vain.

It is in vain that you rise up early and go late to rest, eating the bread of anxious toil; for [the LORD] gives sleep to his beloved.

130 Out of the depths I cry to you, O LORD.

Lord, hear my voice! Let your ears be attentive to the voice of my supplications!

If you, O LORD, should mark iniquities, Lord, who could stand? But there is forgiveness with you, so that you may be revered.

I wait for the LORD, my soul waits, and in his word I hope; my soul waits for the Lord more than those who watch for the morning.

Hope in the LORD! For with the LORD there is steadfast love, and with him is great power to redeem.

131 O LORD, my heart is not proud, nor haughty my eyes; I do not occupy myself with things too great and too marvellous for me.

I have stilled and quieted my soul; like a weaned child with its mother, like a weaned child is my soul within me.

139 O LORD, you have searched me and known me.

You know when I sit down and when I rise up; you discern my thoughts from far away … and are acquainted with all my ways.

Even before a word is on my tongue, O LORD, you know it completely.

You hem me in, behind and before, and lay your hand upon me.

Such knowledge is too wonderful for me; it is so high that I cannot attain it.

Where can I go from your spirit? Or where can I flee from your presence? If I ascend to heaven, you are there; if I make my bed in the depths, you are there.

If I rise on the wings of the dawn, if I settle on the far side of the sea, even there your hand will guide me, your right hand will hold me fast.

If I say, "Surely the darkness shall cover me, and the light around me become night," even the darkness is not dark to you; the night is as bright as the day, for darkness is as light to you.

You created my inmost being; you knit me together in my mother's womb.

I praise you, for I am fearfully and wonderfully made.

Your eyes beheld my unformed substance. In your book were written all the days that were formed for me, when none of them as yet existed.

How weighty to me are your thoughts, O God! How vast is the sum of them! I try to count them – they are more than the sand; I come to the end – I am still with you.

Search me, O God, and know my heart; test me and know my thoughts. See if there is any wicked way in me, and lead me in the way everlasting.

143 Answer me quickly, O LORD; my spirit fails. Do not hide your face from me, or I shall be like those who go down to the Pit.

Let me hear of your steadfast love in the morning, for in you I put my trust.

Teach me the way I should go, for to you I lift up my soul.

Teach me to do your will, for you are my God. Let your good spirit lead me on a level path.

145 The LORD is gracious and merciful, slow to anger and abounding in steadfast love.

The LORD is good to all, and his compassion is over all that he has made.

The LORD is faithful in all his words, and gracious in all his deeds.

The LORD upholds all who are falling, and raises up all who are bowed down.

The LORD is just in all his ways, and loving in all his deeds.

The LORD is near to all who call on him, to all who call on him in truth.

The LORD watches over all who love him.

147 The LORD heals the brokenhearted, and binds up their wounds.

148 Praise the LORD! Praise the LORD from the heavens; praise him in the heights!

Praise him, all his angels; praise him, all his host! Praise him, sun and moon; praise him, all you shining stars!

150 Let everything that breathes praise the LORD!

Proverbs

1 The fear of the LORD is the beginning of knowledge.

3 Trust in the LORD with all your heart, and do not rely on your own insight. In all your ways acknowledge him, and he will make straight your paths.

Do not be wise in your own eyes; fear the LORD, and turn away from evil. It will be a healing for your flesh and refreshment for your body.

Honour the LORD with your substance and with the first fruits of all your produce; then your barns will be filled with plenty, and your vats will be bursting with wine.

My child, do not despise the LORD's discipline or be weary of his reproof, for the LORD reproves the one he loves, as a father the son in whom he delights.

Happy are those who find wisdom, and those who get understanding, for her income is better than silver, and her revenue better than gold. She is a tree of life to those who lay hold of her; those who hold her fast are called happy.

Keep sound wisdom and prudence, and they will be life for your soul.

You will walk on your way securely and your foot will not stumble. If you sit down, you will not be afraid; when you lie down, your sleep will be sweet.

Do not be afraid of sudden panic, or of the storm that strikes the wicked; for the LORD will be your confidence and will keep your foot from being caught.

Do not withhold good from those to whom it is due, when it is in your power to do it. Do not say to your neighbour, "Go, and come again, tomorrow I will give it" – when you have it with you.

Do not quarrel with anyone without cause, when no harm has been done to you.

4 'I have led you in the paths of uprightness. When you walk, your step will not be hampered; and if you run, you will not stumble.'

The path of the righteous is like the light of dawn, which shines brighter and brighter until full day.

Keep your heart with all vigilance, for from it flows the springs of life.

Put away from you crooked speech, and put devious talk far from you. Let your eyes look directly forward, and your gaze be straight before you.

5   Drink water from your own cistern, flowing water from your own well. Should your springs be scattered abroad, streams of water in the streets? Let them be for yourself alone, and not for sharing with strangers.

6   Things that the LORD hates: haughty eyes, a lying tongue, and hands that shed innocent blood, a heart that devises wicked plans, feet that hurry to run to evil, a lying witness who testifies falsely, and one who sows discord in a family.

8   Wisdom is better than jewels, and all that you may desire cannot compare with her.

The LORD created me at the beginning of his work, the first of his acts of long ago ... before the beginning of the earth.

When the LORD established the heavens, I was there, when he drew a circle on the face of the deep ... when he marked out the foundations of the earth, then I was beside him, like a master worker ... delighting in the human race.

10   Hatred stirs up strife, but love covers all offences.

Whoever heeds instruction is on the path to life, but one who rejects a rebuke goes astray.

Lying lips conceal hatred, and whoever utters slander is a fool.

When words are many, transgression is not lacking, but the prudent are restrained in speech.

11   When pride comes, then comes disgrace; but wisdom is with the humble.

Whoever belittles another lacks sense, but an intelligent person remains silent.

A gossip goes about telling secrets, but one who is trustworthy in spirit keeps a confidence.

Some give freely, yet grow all the richer; others withhold what is due, and only suffer want.

A generous person will be enriched, and one who gives water will get water.

12 No one finds security by wickedness, but the root of the righteous will never be moved.

Fools think their own way is right, but the wise listen to advice.

Fools show their anger at once, but the prudent ignore an insult.

Rash words are like sword thrusts, but the tongue of the wise brings healing.

One who is clever conceals knowledge, but the mind of a fool broadcasts folly.

Anxiety weighs down the human heart, but a good word cheers it up.

13 A bad messenger brings trouble, but a faithful envoy, healing.

Whoever walks with the wise becomes wise, but the companion of fools suffers harm.

14 Whoever is slow to anger has great understanding, but one who has a hasty temper exalts folly.

A tranquil mind gives life to the flesh, but passion makes the bones rot.

Those who oppress the poor insult their Maker, but those who are kind to the needy honour him.

15 A soft answer turns away wrath, but a harsh word stirs up anger.

A gentle tongue is a tree of life, but perverseness in it breaks the spirit.

A glad heart makes a cheerful countenance, but by sorrow of heart the spirit is broken.

Better is a dinner of vegetables where love is than a fatted ox with hatred.

16 Commit your work to the LORD, and your plans will be established.

The human mind plans the way, but the LORD directs the steps.

A perverse person spreads strife, and a whisperer separates close friends.

One who is slow to anger is better than the mighty, and one whose temper is controlled than one who captures a city.

The lot is cast into the lap, but the decision is the LORD's alone.

17 Those who mock the poor insult their Maker; those who are glad at calamity will not go unpunished.

A cheerful heart is a good medicine, but a downcast spirit dries up the bones.

18 A fool takes no pleasure in understanding, but only in expressing personal opinion.

19 Those with good sense are slow to anger, and it is their glory to overlook an offence.

Whoever is kind to the poor lends to the LORD, and will be repaid in full.

The human mind may devise many plans, but it is the purpose of the LORD that will be established.

The fear of the LORD is life indeed; filled with it one rests secure and suffers no harm.

20 The lazy person does not plough in season; harvest comes, and there is nothing to be found.

Who can say: I have made my heart clean; I am pure from my sin?

21 If you close your ear to the cry of the poor, you will cry out and not be heard.

27 Do not boast about tomorrow, for you do not know what a day may bring.

Let another praise you, and not your own mouth – a stranger, and not your own lips.

Whoever blesses a neighbour with a loud voice, rising early in the morning, will be counted as cursing.

Just as water reflects the face, so one human heart reflects another.

30   Two things I ask of you; do not deny them to me before I die: Remove far from me falsehood and lying; give me neither poverty nor riches;

31   Speak out for those who cannot speak, for the rights of all the destitute. Speak out, judge righteously, defend the rights of the poor and needy.

Ecclesiastes

1   Vanity of vanities ... All is vanity.

What do people gain from all the toil at which they toil under the sun? A generation goes, and a generation comes, but the earth remains forever.

All things are wearisome; more than one can express; the eye is not satisfied with seeing, or the ear filled with hearing.

What has been is what will be, and what has been done is what will be done; there is nothing new under the sun.

For in much wisdom is much vexation, and those who increase knowledge increase sorrow.

2   I said to myself, "Come now, I will make a test of pleasure; enjoy yourself." But again, this also was vanity.

3   For everything there is a season ... a time to be born, and a time to die; ... a time to break down, and a time to build up; ... a time to mourn, and a time to dance; ... a time to seek, and a time to lose; ... a time to keep silence, and a time to speak.

4   I saw all the oppressions that are practised under the sun. Look, the tears of the oppressed – with no one to comfort them!

Then I saw that all toil and all skill in work come from one person's envy of another.

Two are better than one ... for if they fall, one will lift up the other ... if two lie together, they keep warm; but how can one keep warm alone?

5 Sweet is the sleep of labourers, whether they eat little or much; but the surfeit of the rich will not let them sleep.

This is what I have seen to be good: it is fitting to eat and drink and find enjoyment in all the toil with which one toils under the sun the few days of the life God gives us; for this is our lot.

7 In the day of prosperity be joyful, and in the day of adversity consider; God has made the one as well as the other.

Surely there is no one on earth so righteous as to do good without ever sinning.

Do not give heed to everything that people say, or you may hear your servant cursing you; your heart knows that many times you have yourself cursed others.

11 Send out your bread upon the waters, for after many days you will get it back.

Just as you do not know how the breath comes to the bones in the mother's womb, so you do not know the work of God, who makes everything.

The Wisdom of Solomon

1 God did not make death, and he does not delight in the death of the living. For he created all things so that they might exist; the generative forces of the world are wholesome, and there is no destructive poison in them, and the dominion of Hades is not on earth.

2 God created us for incorruption, and made us in the image of his own eternity.

3   The souls of the righteous are in the hand of God, and no torment will ever touch them. In the eyes of the foolish they seemed to have died, and their departure was thought to be a disaster, and their going from us to be their destruction; but they are at peace.

6   Wisdom is radiant and unfading, and she is easily discerned by those who love her, and is found by those who seek her. She hastens to make herself known to those who desire her. One who rises early to seek her will have no difficulty, for she will be found sitting at the gate.

7   Therefore I prayed, and understanding was given me; I called on God, and the spirit of wisdom came to me. I preferred her to sceptres and thrones, and I accounted wealth as nothing in comparison with her.

I loved [Wisdom] more than health and beauty, and I chose to have her rather than light, because her radiance never ceases. All good things came to me along with her, and in her hands uncounted wealth.

9   Who can learn the counsel of God? Or who can discern what the Lord wills? For the reasoning of mortals is worthless, and our designs are likely to fail; for a perishable body weighs down the soul, and this earthy tent burdens the thoughtful mind.

We can hardly guess at what is on earth, and what is at hand we find with labour; but who has traced out what is in the heavens?

11   The whole world before you [O Lord] is like a speck that tips the scales, and like a drop of morning dew that falls on the ground. But you are merciful to all, for you can do all things, and you overlook people's sins, so that they may repent.

You love all things that exist, and detest none of the things that you have made, for you would not have made anything if you had hated it.

How would anything have endured if you had not willed it? Or how would anything not called forth by you have been preserved?

You spare all things, for they are yours, O Lord, you who love the living.

12 Your immortal spirit is in all things. Therefore you correct little by little those who trespass, and you remind and warn them of the things through which they sin, so that they may be freed from wickedness and put their trust in you, O Lord.

You are righteous [O Lord], and you rule all things righteously, deeming it alien to your power to condemn anyone who does not deserve to be punished. For your strength is the source of right-eousness, and your sovereignty over all causes you to spare all.

15 You, our God, are kind and true, patient, and ruling all things in mercy. For even if we sin we are yours, knowing your power; but we will not sin, because we know that you acknowledge us as yours.

Sirach (Ecclesiasticus)

1 The fear of the Lord delights the heart, and gives gladness and joy and long life. Those who fear the Lord will have a happy end; on the day of their death they will be blessed.

Those who are patient stay calm until the right moment, and then cheerfulness comes back to them. They hold back their words until the right moment; then the lips of many tell of their good sense.

2 Trust in God, and he will help you; make your ways straight, and hope in him.

The Lord is compassionate and merciful; he forgives sins and saves in time of distress.

3 Those who honour their father atone for sins, and those who respect their mother are like those who lay up treasure.

My child, help your father in his old age, and do not grieve him as long as he lives; even if his mind fails, be patient with him; because you have all your faculties do not despise him. For kindness to a father will not be forgotten, and will be credited to you against your sins; in the day of your distress it will be remembered in your favour; like frost in fair weather, your sins will melt away.

The greater you are, the more you must humble yourself; so you will find favour in the sight of the Lord.

As water extinguishes a blazing fire, so almsgiving atones for sin.

4   My child, do not cheat the poor of their living, and do not keep needy eyes waiting. Do not grieve the hungry, or anger one in need.

Do not add to the troubles of the desperate, or delay giving to the needy. Do not reject a suppliant in distress, or turn your face away from the poor.

Be a father to orphans, and be like a husband to their mother; you will then be like a son of the Most High, and he will love you more than does your mother.

Do not refrain from speaking at the proper moment, and do not hide your wisdom. For wisdom becomes known through speech, and education through the words of the tongue.

Fight to the death for truth, and the Lord God will fight for you.

Do not let your hand be stretched out to receive and closed when it is time to give.

6   Let those who are friendly with you be many, but let your advisers be one in a thousand.

Faithful friends are a sturdy shelter: whoever finds one has found a treasure. Faithful friends are beyond price; no amount can balance their worth.

7   Do not grow weary when you pray; do not neglect to give alms.

Stretch out your hand to the poor, so that your blessing may be complete. Give graciously to all the living; do not withhold kindness even from the dead.

Do not avoid those who weep, but mourn with those who mourn.

Do not hesitate to visit the sick, because for such deeds you will be loved.

In all you do, remember the end of your life, and then you will never sin.

11   Do not find fault before you investigate; examine first, and then criticize. Do not answer before you listen, and do not interrupt when another is speaking.

15   It was God who created humankind in the beginning, and he left them in the power of their own free choice. If you choose, you can keep the commandments, and to act faithfully is a matter of your own choice.

17   To those who repent he grants a return, and he encourages those who are losing hope.

Turn back to the Lord and forsake your sins; pray in his presence and lessen your offence.

How great is the mercy of the Lord, and his forgiveness for those who return to him!

18   What are human beings, and of what use are they? What is good in them, and what is evil? The number of days in their life is great if they reach one hundred years. Like a drop of water from the sea and a grain of sand, so are a few years among the days of eternity. That is why the Lord is patient with them and pours out his mercy upon them. He sees and recognizes that their end is miserable; therefore he grants them forgiveness all the more.

The compassion of human beings is for their neighbours, but the compassion of the Lord is for every living thing. He rebukes and trains and teaches them, and turns them back, as a shepherd his flock.

My child, do not mix reproach with your good deeds, or spoil your gift by harsh words. Does not the dew give relief from the scorching heat? So a word is better than a gift. Indeed, does not a word surpass a good gift? Both are to be found in a gracious person.

19   Never repeat a conversation, and you will lose nothing at all. With friend or foe do not report it, and unless it would be a sin for you, do not reveal it.

Have you heard something? Let it die with you. Be brave, it will not make you burst!

Question a friend; perhaps he did not do it; or if he did, so that he may not do it again. Question a neighbour; perhaps he did not say it; or if he said it, so that he may not repeat it. Question a friend, for often it is slander; so do not believe everything you hear. A person may make a slip without intending it. Who has not sinned with his tongue?

20   Some people keep silent and are thought to be wise, while others are detested for being talkative. Some people keep silent because they have nothing to say, while others keep silent because they know when to speak.

21   The prayer of the poor goes from their lips to the ears of God, and his judgment comes speedily.

25   I take pleasure in three things, and they are beautiful in the sight of God and of mortals: agreement among brothers and sisters, friendship among neighbours, and a wife and a husband who live in harmony.

How attractive is wisdom in the aged, and understanding and counsel in the venerable! Rich experience is the crown of the aged, and their boast is the fear of the Lord.

28   The vengeful will face the Lord's vengeance, for he keeps a strict account of their sins. Forgive your neighbour the wrong he has done, and then your sins will be pardoned when you pray.

Does anyone harbour anger against another, and expect healing from the Lord? If one has no mercy toward another like himself, can he then seek pardon for his own sins?

29   The merciful lend to their neighbours; by holding out a helping hand they keep the commandments. Lend to your neighbour in his

time of need; repay your neighbour when a loan falls due.

Be patient with someone in humble circumstances, and do not keep him waiting for your alms. Help the poor for the commandment's sake, and in their need do not send them away empty-handed.

The necessities of life are water, bread, and clothing, and also a house to assure privacy. Better is the life of the poor under their own crude roof than sumptuous food in the house of others.

30   A joyful heart is life itself, and rejoicing lengthens one's life span. Indulge yourself and take comfort, and remove sorrow far from you, for sorrow has destroyed many, and no advantage ever comes from it.

Jealousy and anger shorten life, and anxiety brings on premature old age. Those who are cheerful and merry at table will benefit from their food.

31   Wakefulness over wealth wastes away one's flesh, and anxiety about it drives away sleep.

In everything you do be moderate, and no sickness will overtake you.

Wine is very life to human beings if taken in moderation. What is life to one who is without wine? It has been created to make people happy. Wine drunk at the proper time and in moderation is rejoicing of heart and gladness of soul. Wine drunk to excess leads to bitterness of spirit, to quarrels and stumbling.

32   The one who seeks God will accept his discipline, and those who rise early to seek him will find favour.

Do nothing without deliberation, but when you have acted, do not regret it.

33   Like clay in the hand of the potter, to be moulded as he pleases, so all are in the hand of their Maker, to be given whatever he decides.

34 The eyes of the Lord are on those who love him, a mighty shield and strong support, a shelter from scorching wind and a shade from noonday sun, a guard against stumbling and a help against falling.

The Lord lifts up the soul and makes the eyes sparkle; he gives health and life and blessing.

To take away a neighbour's living is to commit murder; to deprive an employee of wages is to shed blood.

35 The Lord is the judge, and with him there is no partiality. He will not show partiality to the poor; but he will listen to the prayer of one who is wronged. He will not ignore the supplication of the orphan, or the widow when she pours out her complaint.

The prayer of the humble pierces the clouds, and it will not rest until it reaches its goal; it will not desist until the Most High responds and does justice for the righteous, and executes judgment.

39 He sets his heart to rise early to seek the Lord who made him, and to petition the Most High; he opens his mouth in prayer and asks pardon for his sins.

40 Hard work was created for everyone, and a heavy yoke is laid on the children of Adam from the day they come forth from their mother's womb until the day they return to the mother of all the living.

Perplexities and fear of heart are theirs, and anxious thought of the day of their death. From the one who sits on a splendid throne to the one who grovels in dust and ashes ... there is anger and envy and trouble and unrest, and fear of death, and fury and strife.

Kindness is like a garden of blessings, and almsgiving endures forever.

Wine and music gladden the heart, but the love of friends is better than either.

41   O death, how bitter is the thought of you to the one at peace among possessions, who has nothing to worry about and is prosperous in everything, and still is vigorous enough to enjoy food!

O death, how welcome is your sentence to one who is needy and failing in strength, worn down by age and anxious about everything; to one who is contrary, and has lost all patience!

3. PROPHECY:
Words as Exhortation
and Encouragement

The prophets, in Old Testament terms, are not so much foretelling the future for their listeners as demanding a change of behaviour in the present so that they can *change* the future. There is an enormous range of tone in these writings, stretching from heroic enthusiasm and warm encouragement to petty threats and moral blackmail. Sometimes the transparency of the latter, with its all-too-human face, is almost comical as the writers picture God urging His people to return to Him in one chapter and cursing them in the next. But a couple of things might be borne in mind: firstly, it appears that these men undertook their roles with great reluctance, unlike many latter-day religious leaders; and, secondly, they saw themselves as *inside* the community they were criticizing, not 'holy outsiders' telling 'sinners' what to do. In the end the prophetic vocation was a sign of an entire people involved in constant self-correction and growth, trying to respond adequately to God by keeping His laws, especially those involving justice, mercy, forgiveness and peace. The prophets' radical vision of economic and social equality remains a serious challenge to readers in every age.

Isaiah

1   'Wash yourselves; make yourselves clean; remove the evil of your doings from before my eyes; cease to do evil, learn to do good.'

'Come now, let us argue it out', says the LORD: 'though your sins are like scarlet, they shall be like snow; though they are red like crimson, they shall become like wool.'

2   Many peoples shall come and say: Come, let us go up to the mountain of the LORD, to the house of the God of Jacob; that he may teach us his ways and that we may walk in his paths.

   They shall beat their swords into ploughshares, and their spears into pruning hooks; nation shall not lift up sword against nation, neither shall they learn war any more.

5   My beloved had a vineyard on a very fertile hill … he expected it to yield grapes, but it yielded wild grapes. What more was there to do for my vineyard that I have not done in it?

6   I heard the voice of the Lord saying, 'Whom shall I send, and who will go for us?' And I said: "Here am I; send me!"

7   The Lord himself will give you a sign. Look, the young woman is with child and shall bear a son, and shall name him Immanuel.

9   The people who walked in darkness have seen a great light; those who lived in a land of deep darkness – on them light has shone.

   The yoke of their burden, and the bar across their shoulders, the rod of their oppressor, you have broken.

   For a child has been born for us, a son given to us; authority rests upon his shoulders; and he is named Wonderful Counsellor, Mighty God, Everlasting Father, Prince of Peace.

11 A shoot shall come out from the stump of Jesse, and a branch shall grow out of his roots. The spirit of the LORD shall rest on him, the spirit of wisdom and understanding, the spirit of counsel and might, the spirit of knowledge and the fear of the LORD.

12 Surely God is my salvation; I will trust, and will not be afraid.

25 On this mountain the LORD of hosts will make for all peoples a feast of rich food, a feast of well-aged wines, of rich food filled with marrow, of well-aged wines strained clear.

   The LORD will destroy on this mountain the shroud that is cast over all peoples, the sheet that is spread over all nations; he will swallow up death forever.

The Lord GOD will wipe away the tears from all faces, and the disgrace of his people he will take away from all the earth, for the LORD has spoken.

26   Your dead shall live, their corpses shall rise. O dwellers in the dust, awake and sing for joy! For your dew is a radiant dew, and the earth will give birth to those long dead.

27   A pleasant vineyard, sing about it! 'I, the LORD, am its keeper; every moment I water it. I guard it night and day so that no one can harm it; I have no wrath … Let it cling to me for protection, let it make peace with me.'

29   'These people draw near with their mouths and honour me with their lips, while their hearts are far from me, and their worship of me is a human commandment learned by rote.'

'Shall the potter be regarded as the clay? Shall the thing made say of its maker: "He did not make me"; or the thing formed say of the one who formed it: "He has no understanding"?'

30   'In returning and rest you shall be saved; in quietness and in trust shall be your strength.'

The LORD waits to be gracious to you; therefore he will rise up to show mercy to you. For the LORD is a God of justice; blessed are all those who wait for him.

You shall weep no more. How gracious he will be when you cry for help! As soon as he hears, he will answer you.

Whether you turn to the right or to the left, your ears will hear a voice behind you, saying: This is the way; walk in it.

33   O LORD, be gracious to us; we wait for you. Be our arm every morning, our salvation in the time of trouble.

35   Strengthen the weak hands, and make firm the feeble knees. Say to

those who are of a fearful heart: Be strong, do not fear! Here is your God ... He will come and save you.

Then the eyes of the blind shall be opened, and the ears of the deaf unstopped; then the lame shall leap like a deer, and the tongue of the speechless sing for joy.

40 'Comfort, O comfort my people', says your God. 'Speak tenderly to Jerusalem, and cry to her that she has served her term, that her penalty is paid.'

A voice cries out: In the wilderness prepare the way of the LORD, make straight in the desert a highway for our God. Every valley shall be lifted up, and every mountain and hill be made low; the uneven ground shall become level, and the rough places a plain.

All flesh is grass, and all its beauty is like the flower of the field. The grass withers, the flower fades; but the word of our God will stand forever.

The Lord GOD will feed his flock like a shepherd; he will gather the lambs in his arms, and carry them in his bosom, and gently lead the mother sheep.

Who has measured the waters in the hollow of his hand and marked off the heavens with a span, enclosed the dust of the earth in a measure, and weighed the mountains in scales and the hills in a balance?

Who has directed the spirit of the LORD, or as his counsellor has instructed him? Whom did he consult for his enlightenment, and who taught him the path of justice? Who taught him knowledge, and showed him the way of understanding?

The LORD is the everlasting God, the Creator of the ends of the earth. He does not faint or grow weary; his understanding is unsearchable.

Even youths will faint and be weary, and the young will fall exhausted; but those who wait for the LORD shall renew their strength, they shall mount up with wings like eagles, they shall run and not be weary, they shall walk and not faint.

41 'Do not fear, for I am with you, do not be afraid, for I am your God.'

'I, the LORD your God, hold your right hand; it is I who say to you: Do not fear, I will help you.'

'When the poor and needy seek water, and there is none, and their tongue is parched with thirst, I the LORD will answer them, I the God of Israel will not forsake them.'

42 'Here is my servant, whom I uphold, my chosen, in whom my soul delights.'

'I have put my spirit upon him; he will bring forth justice to the nations.'

'He will not cry or lift up his voice, or make it heard in the street; a bruised reed he will not break, and a dimly burning wick he will not quench.'

'I am the LORD, I have called you in righteousness, I have taken you by the hand and kept you.'

'I have given you as a covenant to the people, a light to the nations, to open the eyes that are blind, to bring out the prisoners from the dungeon, from the prison those who sit in darkness.'

'I will lead the blind by a road they do not know, by paths they have not known I will guide them. I will turn the darkness before them into light, the rough places into level ground … I will not forsake them.'

43 Thus says the LORD, he who created you … 'Do not fear, for I have redeemed you; I have called you by name, you are mine.'

'When you pass through the waters, I will be with you; and through the rivers, they shall not overwhelm you; when you walk through fire you shall not be burned, and the flame shall not consume you.'

'I am the LORD your God ... you are precious in my sight, and honoured, and I love you.'

'Do not fear, for I am with you.'

'You have burdened me with your sins; you have wearied me with your iniquities. I, I am He who blots out your transgressions for my own sake, and I will not remember your sins.'

44 Thus says the LORD who made you, who formed you in the womb and will help you: 'Do not fear.'

'I am the first and I am the last; besides me there is no god.'

'I formed you, you are my servant ... I have swept away your transgressions like a cloud, and your sins like mist.'

'Return to me, for I have redeemed you.'

45 'Turn to me and be saved, all the ends of the earth! For I am God, and there is no other ... to me every knee shall bow, every tongue shall swear.'

46 'Listen to me ... who have been borne by me from your birth, carried from the womb; even to your old age I am he, even when you turn grey I will carry you.'

'I have made, and I will bear; I will carry and will save.'

49 The LORD called me before I was born, while I was in my mother's womb he named me ... in the shadow of his hand he hid me.

'In a time of favour I have answered you, on a day of salvation I have helped you ... Say to the prisoners: Come out; say to those who are in darkness: Show yourselves.'

Sing for joy, O heavens, and exult, O earth; break forth, O mountains, into singing! For the LORD has comforted his people, and will have compassion on his suffering ones.

'[You say] "The LORD has forsaken me, my Lord has forgotten me." Can a woman forget her nursing child, or show no compassion for the child of her womb? Even these may forget, yet I will not forget you. See, I have inscribed you on the palms of my hands.'

53 He was despised and rejected; a man of suffering and acquainted with infirmity; and as one from whom others hide their faces he was despised, and we held him of no account.

Surely he has borne our infirmities and carried our diseases.

He was wounded for our transgressions, crushed for our iniquities; upon him was the punishment that made us whole, and by his bruises we are healed.

All we like sheep have gone astray; we have all turned to our own way, and the LORD has laid on him the iniquity of us all.

By a perversion of justice he was taken away. Who could have imagined his future? For he was cut off from the land of the living, stricken for the transgression of my people.

The righteous one, my servant, shall make many righteous, and he shall bear their iniquities.

Therefore I will allot him a portion with the great, and he shall divide the spoil with the strong; because he poured out himself to death, and was numbered with the transgressors; yet he bore the sin of many, and made intercession for the transgressors.

54 'For a brief moment I abandoned you, but with great compassion I will gather you … with everlasting love I will have compassion on you', says the LORD, your Redeemer.

'For the mountains may depart and the hills be removed, but my steadfast love shall not depart from you, and my covenant of peace shall not be removed', says the LORD, who has compassion on you.

55 Ho, everyone who thirsts, come to the waters; and you that have no money, come, buy and eat! Come, buy wine and milk without money and without price.

Why do you spend your money for that which is not bread, and your labour for that which does not satisfy? Listen carefully to me, and eat what is good, and delight yourselves in rich food.

Seek the LORD while he may be found, call upon him while he is near.

Let the wicked forsake their way, and the unrighteous their thoughts; let them return to the LORD, that he may have mercy on them, and to our God, for he will abundantly pardon.

'My thoughts are not your thoughts, nor are your ways my ways', says the LORD. 'For as the heavens are higher than the earth, so are my ways higher than your ways and my thoughts than your thoughts.'

57 'I will not continually accuse, nor will I always be angry; for then the spirits would grow faint before me, even the souls that I have made.'

'I will heal them; I will lead them and repay them with comfort.'

'Peace, peace, to the far and the near ... I will heal them.'

58 'Is not this the fast that I choose: to loose the bonds of injustice, to undo the thongs of the yoke, to let the oppressed go free, and to break every yoke? Is it not to share your bread with the hungry, and bring the homeless poor into your house; when you see the naked, to cover them, and not to hide yourself from your own kin?'

'If you remove the yoke from among you, the pointing of the finger, the speaking of evil, if you offer your food to the hungry and satisfy the needs of the afflicted, then your light shall rise in the darkness and your gloom be like the noonday.'

60 Arise, shine; for your light has come, and the glory of the LORD has risen upon you. For darkness shall cover the earth, and thick darkness the peoples; but the LORD will arise upon you, and his glory will appear over you.

'The sun shall no longer be your light by day, nor for brightness shall the moon give light to you by night; but the LORD will be your everlasting light, and your God will be your glory ... your days of mourning shall be ended.'

61   The spirit of the Lord GOD is upon me, because the LORD has anointed me; he has sent me to bring good news to the oppressed, to bind up the brokenhearted, to proclaim liberty to the captives, and release to the prisoners; to proclaim the year of the Lord's favour.

62   You shall no more be termed Forsaken, and your land shall no more be termed Desolate; but you shall be called My Delight Is in Her, and your land Married; for the LORD delights in you … as the bridegroom rejoices over the bride, so shall your God rejoice over you.

63   The LORD became their saviour in all their distress. It was no messenger or angel but his presence that saved them; in his love and in his pity he redeemed them; he lifted them up and carried them.

64   O LORD, you are our Father; we are the clay, you are the potter; we are all the work of your hand.

65   'I revealed myself to those who did not ask for me; I was found by those who did not seek me. To a nation that did not call on my name, I said: Here am I, here am I.'

       'I am about to create new heavens and a new earth; the former things shall not be remembered or come to mind.'

66   'As a mother comforts her child, so I will comfort you.'

       'From new moon to new moon, and from sabbath to sabbath, all flesh shall come to worship before me.'

Jeremiah

1   'Before I formed you in the womb I knew you, and before you were born I consecrated you.'

       "Ah, Lord GOD! Truly I do not know how to speak, for I am only a boy." But the LORD said to me, 'Do not say: I am only a boy; for you shall go to all to whom I send you, and you shall speak whatever I command you, Do not be afraid of them, for I am with you to deliver you.'

Then the LORD put out his hand and touched my mouth; and the LORD said to me, 'Now I have put my words in your mouth.'

2   'Be appalled, O heavens, at this, be shocked, be utterly desolate', says the LORD, 'for my people have committed two evils: they have forsaken me, the fountain of living water, and dug out cisterns for themselves, cracked cisterns that can hold no water.'

3   'I will give you shepherds after my own heart, who will feed you with knowledge and understanding.'

'I thought how I would set you among my children, and give you a pleasant land, the most beautiful heritage of all the nations. And I thought you would call me, My Father, and would not turn from following me.'

'Instead, as a faithless wife leaves her husband, so you have been faithless to me, O house of Israel ... Return, O faithless children, I will heal your faithlessness.'

12   You, O LORD, know me; you see me and test me – my heart is with you.

14   You, O LORD, are in the midst of us, and we are called by your name; do not forsake us!

17   Blessed is the one who trusts in the LORD, whose confidence is in him. That person shall be like a tree planted by the water, that sends out its roots by the stream. It shall not fear when heat comes; its leaves shall stay green; in the year of drought it is not anxious, and it does not cease to bear fruit.

18   'Just like the clay in the potter's hand, so are you in my hand, O house of Israel.'

20   LORD, you have enticed me, and I was enticed; you have overpowered me, and you have prevailed.

The word of the LORD has become for me a reproach and derision all day long. If I say, "I will not mention him, or speak any more in his name," then within me there is something like a burning fire shut up in my bones; I am weary with holding it in, and I cannot.

22 'Woe to him who builds his house by unrighteousness, and his upper rooms by injustice; who makes his neighbours work for nothing, and does not give them their wages.'

23 'Woe to the shepherds who destroy and scatter the sheep of my pasture!'

'I myself will gather the remnant of my flock out of all the lands where I have driven them, and I will bring them back to their fold, and they shall be fruitful and multiply.'

'I will raise up shepherds over them who will shepherd them, and they shall not fear any longer, or be dismayed, nor shall any be missing.'

24 'I will give them a heart to know that I am the LORD; and they shall be my people and I will be their God, for they shall return to me with their whole heart.'

29 'When you call upon me and come and pray to me, I will hear you. When you search for me, you will find me; if you seek me with all your heart.'

30 'Have no fear … and do not be dismayed … I am with you to save you.'

'I will restore health to you, and your wounds I will heal; and you shall be my people, and I will be your God.'

31 'I have loved you with an everlasting love; therefore I have contin-ued my faithfulness to you.'

'I will turn their mourning into joy, I will comfort them, and give them gladness for sorrow.'

'I will satisfy the weary, and all who are faint I will refresh.'

'No longer shall they teach one another, or say to each other: Know the LORD; for they shall all know me, from the least of them to the greatest.'

Lamentations

1   Look, O LORD, and see how worthless I have become. Is it nothing to you, all you who pass by? Look and see if there is any sorrow like my sorrow.

2   Give yourself no rest, your eyes no respite! Arise, cry out in the night, at the beginning of the watches! Pour out your heart like water before the presence of the Lord!

3   My soul is bereft of peace; I have forgotten what happiness is.

     But this I call to mind, and therefore I have hope: The steadfast love of the LORD never ceases, his mercies never come to an end; they are new every morning; great is your faithfulness.

     The LORD is good to those who wait for him, to the soul that seeks him.

     It is good that one should wait quietly for the salvation of the LORD.

Ezekiel

11   'I will give them one heart, and put a new spirit within them; I will remove from them their heart of stone and give them a heart of flesh, so that they may follow my statutes and keep my ordinances and obey them.'

18   'A child shall not suffer for the iniquity of a parent, nor a parent suffer for the iniquity of a child; the righteousness of the righteous shall be his own, and the wickedness of the wicked shall be his own.'

     'If the wicked turn away from all their sins that they have committed ... none of the transgressions that they have committed shall be remembered against them.'

'Cast away from you all the transgressions that you have committed against me, and get yourselves a new heart and a new spirit!'

34 'Ah, you shepherds of Israel ... you have not strengthened the weak, you have not healed the sick, you have not bound up the injured, you have not brought back the strayed, you have not sought the lost, but with force and harshness you have ruled them.'

'My sheep were scattered, they wandered over all the mountains and on every high hill; my sheep were scattered over all the face of the earth, with no one to search or seek for them.'

'I myself will search for my sheep, and will seek them out ... I will rescue them from all the places to which they have been scattered on a day of clouds and thick darkness.'

'I will feed them with good pasture ... I myself will be the shepherd of my sheep, and I will make them lie down ... I will seek the lost, and I will bring back the strayed, and I will bind up the injured, and I will strengthen the weak.'

'They shall live in safety, and no one shall make them afraid ... they shall know that I, the LORD their God, am with them, and that they, the house of Israel, are my people.'

36 'I am for you; I will turn to you ... and will do more good to you than ever before. Then you shall know that I am the LORD.'

'I will sprinkle clean water upon you, and you shall be clean from all your uncleanness, and from all your idols I will cleanse you. A new heart I will give you, and a new spirit I will put within you; and I will remove from your body the heart of stone and give you a heart of flesh.'

37 O dry bones, hear the word of the LORD: ... 'I will cause breath to enter you, and you shall live. I will lay sinews on you, and will cause flesh to come upon you, and cover you with skin, and put breath in you, and you shall live.'

'I am going to open your graves, and bring you up from your graves ... I will put my spirit within you, and you shall live.'

Hosea

2   'I will take you for my wife forever; I will take you for my wife in righteousness and in justice, in steadfast love, and in mercy.'

11   'It was I who taught Ephraim to walk, I took them up in my arms; but they did not know that it was I who healed them.'

'I led them with cords of human kindness, with bands of love. I was to them like those who lift infants to their cheeks. I bent down to them and fed them.'

12   Return to your God, hold fast to love and justice, and wait continually for your God.

Joel

2   'Return to me with all your heart, with fasting, with weeping, and with mourning; rend your hearts and not your garments.'

'Return to the LORD, your God, for he is gracious and merciful, slow to anger, and abounding in steadfast love, and relents from punishing.'

'I will pour out my spirit on all flesh; your sons and your daughters shall prophesy, your old men shall dream dreams, and your young men shall see visions.'

'Then everyone who calls on the name of the LORD shall be saved'.

Micah

4   Many nations shall come and say: Come, let us go up to the mountain of the LORD, to the house of the God of Jacob; that he may teach us his ways and that we may walk in his paths.

They shall beat their swords into ploughshares, and their spears into pruning hooks; nation shall not lift up sword against nation, neither shall they learn war any more.

6　What does the LORD require of you but to do justice, and to love kindness, and to walk humbly with your God?

7　When I sit in darkness, the LORD will be a light to me.

He will again have compassion upon us; he will tread our iniquities under foot, and will cast all our sins into the depths of the sea.

Zechariah

2　'Truly, one who touches you touches the apple of my eye.'

8　In those days ten men from nations of every language shall take hold of a Jew, grasping his garment and saying: Let us go with you, for we have heard that God is with you.

Malachi

2　Have we not all one father? Has not one God created us? Why then are we faithless to one another?

New Testament

4. BIOGRAPHY:
Words about and
from the Word

The Gospels are four accounts of the life of Jesus in which, like reading four newspapers reporting on the same events, we can see a fuller portrait than if we were to read one, more complete text. The *Acts of the Apostles* continues the story, describing life in the early Christian community after the resurrection and ascension of Christ. This is not the place to discuss the controversies which have raged through the centuries up to the present day about the dating or authorship of the Gospels. Suffice to say that Matthew, Mark and Luke are known as the Synoptic Gospels ('synoptic' literally meaning 'seen together') because there is much which is common to all three, even some passages exactly duplicated; and John's Gospel was probably written some decades later in a very different, less Hebraic style. Christ's teaching in the Synoptics, with the exception of the 'Sermon on the Mount', tends to be through parables and short conversations, whereas in John there are no parables, and the speeches are often lengthier set pieces imbued with philosophical or mystical significance. Miracles in the Synoptics occur as if they are a spontaneous response to needs met along the way; but in John they are described as 'signs',[17] as if for a predetermined, didactic purpose. Because I wanted to avoid as much repetition as possible, there are parts of the Synoptic Gospels which I have joined together into one narrative, although in every instance it is clearly shown in a footnote what has been done.

---

17. See John 4: 54 and 6: 26.

Matthew

1   Jacob the father of Joseph the husband of Mary, of whom Jesus was born, who is called the Messiah.

When his mother Mary had been engaged to Joseph, but before they lived together, she was found to be with child from the Holy Spirit.

[The angel said], "Joseph, son of David, do not be afraid to take Mary as your wife, for the child conceived in her is from the Holy Spirit."

"She will bear a son, and you are to name him Jesus, for he will save his people from their sins."

All this took place to fulfil what had been spoken by the Lord through the prophet: *Look, the virgin shall conceive and bear a son, and they shall name him Emmanuel*, which means, God is with us.

3   John the Baptist appeared in the wilderness of Judea, proclaiming, "Repent, for the kingdom of heaven has come near."

[John] is the one of whom the prophet Isaiah spoke when he said: *The voice of one crying out in the wilderness: "Prepare the way of the Lord, make his paths straight."*

When Jesus had been baptized [by John], just as he came up from the water, suddenly the heavens were opened to him and he saw the Spirit of God descending like a dove and alighting on him.

A voice from heaven said, 'This is my Son, the Beloved, with whom I am well pleased.'

4   Then Jesus was led up by the Spirit into the wilderness to be tempted by the devil. He fasted for forty days and forty nights, and afterwards he was famished.

The tempter came and said to Jesus, "If you are the Son of God, command these stones to become loaves of bread." But he answered, 'It is written: *One does not live by bread alone, but by every word that comes from the mouth of God.*'

Then the devil took him to the holy city and placed him on the pinnacle of the temple, saying to him, "If you are the Son of God, throw yourself down; for it is written, *He will command his angels concerning you*; and *On their hands they will bear you up, so that you will not dash your foot against a stone.*" Jesus said to him, 'Again it is written, *Do not put the Lord your God to the test.*'

Again, the devil took him to a very high mountain and showed him all the kingdoms of the world and their splendour; and he said to him, "All these I will give you, if you will fall down and worship me." Jesus said to him, 'Away with you, Satan! for it is written, *Worship the Lord your God, and serve only him.*'

5 'Blessed are the poor in spirit, for theirs is the kingdom of heaven.'

'Blessed are those who mourn, for they will be comforted.'

'Blessed are the meek, for they will inherit the earth.'

'Blessed are those who hunger and thirst for righteousness, for they will be filled.'

'Blessed are the merciful, for they will receive mercy.'

'Blessed are the pure in heart, for they will see God.'

'Blessed are the peacemakers, for they will be called children of God.'

'Blessed are those who are persecuted for righteousness' sake, for theirs is the kingdom of heaven.'

'Blessed are you when people revile you and persecute you and utter all kinds of evil against you falsely on my account. Rejoice and be glad, for your reward is great in heaven, for in the same way they persecuted the prophets who were before you.'

'You are the salt of the earth; but if salt has lost its taste, how can its saltiness be restored? It is no longer good for anything, but is thrown out and trampled under foot.'

'You are the light of the world. A city built on a hill cannot be hidden. No one after lighting a lamp puts it under the bushel basket, but on the lampstand, and it gives light to all in the house.'

'In the same way, let your light shine before others, so that they may see your good works and give glory to your Father in heaven.'

'Do not think that I have come to abolish the law or the prophets; I have come not to abolish but to fulfil. For truly I tell you, until heaven and earth pass away, not one letter, not one stroke of a letter, will pass from the law until all is accomplished.'

'Therefore, whoever breaks one of the least of these commandments, and teaches others to do the same, will be called least in the kingdom of heaven; but whoever does them and teaches them will be called great in the kingdom of heaven.'

'For I tell you, unless your righteousness exceeds that of the scribes and Pharisees, you will never enter the kingdom of heaven.'

'You have heard that it was said to those of ancient times: *You shall not murder*; and *whoever murders shall be liable to judgement*. But I say to you that if you are angry with a brother or sister, you will be liable to judgement.'

'So when you are offering your gift at the altar, if you remember that your brother or sister has something against you, leave your gift there before the altar and go; first be reconciled to your brother or sister, and then come and offer your gift.'

'You have heard that it was said, *You shall not commit adultery*. But I say to you that everyone who looks at a woman with lust has already committed adultery with her in his heart.'

'If your right eye causes you to sin, tear it out and throw it away; it is better for you to lose one of your members than for your whole body to be thrown into hell.'

'And if your right hand causes you to sin, cut it off and throw it away; it is better for you to lose one of your members than for your whole body to go into hell.'

'It was also said: *Whoever divorces his wife, let him give her a certificate of divorce*. But I say to you that anyone who divorces his wife, except on the ground of unchastity, causes her to commit adultery; and whoever marries a divorced woman commits adultery.'

'Again, you have heard that it was said to those of ancient times: *You shall not swear falsely, but carry out the vows you have made to the Lord*. But I say to you, Do not swear at all … Let your word be "Yes, Yes" or "No, No"; anything more than this comes from the evil one.'

'You have heard that it was said: *An eye for an eye and a tooth for a tooth*. But I say to you, Do not resist an evildoer. But if anyone strikes you on the right cheek, turn the other also.'

'If anyone wants to sue you and take your coat, give your cloak as well; and if anyone forces you to go one mile, go also the second mile. Give to everyone who begs from you, and do not refuse anyone who wants to borrow from you.'

'You have heard that it was said: *You shall love your neighbour and hate your enemy*. But I say to you, Love your enemies and pray for those who persecute you, so that you may be children of your Father in heaven; for he makes his sun rise on the evil and on the good, and sends rain on the righteous and on the unrighteous.'

'If you love those who love you, what reward do you have? Do not even the tax collectors do the same? And if you greet only your brothers and sisters, what more are you doing than others? Do not even the Gentiles do the same?'

'Be perfect, therefore, as your heavenly Father is perfect.'

6 'Beware of practising your piety before others in order to be seen by them; for then you have no reward from your Father in heaven.'

'Whenever you give alms, do not sound a trumpet before you, as the hypocrites do in the synagogues and in the streets, so that they may be praised by others. Truly I tell you, they have received their reward. But when you give alms, do not let your left hand know what your right hand is doing, so that your alms may be done in secret; and your Father who sees in secret will reward you.'

'Whenever you pray, do not be like the hypocrites; for they love to stand and pray in the synagogues and at the street corners, so that they may be seen by others. Truly I tell you, they have received their reward. But whenever you pray, go into your room and shut the door and pray to your Father who is in secret; and your Father who sees in secret will reward you.'

'When you are praying, do not heap up empty phrases as the Gentiles do; for they think that they will be heard because of their many words. Do not be like them, for your Father knows what you need before you ask him.'

'Pray then in this way: Our Father in heaven, hallowed be your name.'

'Your kingdom come.'

'Your will be done, on earth as it is in heaven.'

'Give us this day our daily bread.'

'Forgive us our debts, as we also have forgiven our debtors.'

'Do not bring us to the time of trial, but rescue us from the evil one.'

'If you forgive others their trespasses, your heavenly Father will also forgive you; but if you do not forgive others, neither will your Father forgive your trespasses.'

'Whenever you fast, do not look dismal, like the hypocrites, for they disfigure their faces so as to show others that they are fasting. Truly I tell you, they have received their reward.'

'When you fast, put oil on your head and wash your face, so that your fasting may be seen not by others but by your Father who is in secret; and your Father who sees in secret will reward you.'

'Do not store up for yourselves treasures on earth, where moth and rust consume and where thieves break in and steal; but store up for yourselves treasures in heaven, where neither moth nor rust consumes and where thieves do not break in and steal. For where your treasure is, there your heart will be also.'

'The eye is the lamp of the body. So, if your eye is healthy, your whole body will be full of light; but if your eye is unhealthy, your whole body will be full of darkness. If then the light in you is darkness, how great is the darkness!'

'No one can serve two masters; for a slave will either hate the one and love the other, or be devoted to the one and despise the other. You cannot serve God and wealth.'

'Therefore I tell you, do not worry about your life, what you will eat or what you will drink, or about your body, what you will wear. Is not life more than food, and the body more than clothing?'

'Look at the birds of the air; they neither sow nor reap nor gather into barns, and yet your heavenly Father feeds them. Are you not of more value than they?'

'Can any of you by worrying add a single hour to your span of life?'

'Why do you worry about clothing? Consider the lilies of the field, how they grow; they neither toil nor spin, yet I tell you, even Solomon in all his glory was not clothed like one of these. But if God so clothes the grass of the field, which is alive today and tomorrow is thrown into the oven, will he not much more clothe you – you of little faith?'

'Therefore do not worry, saying, "What will we eat?" or "What will we drink?" or "What will we wear?" For it is the Gentiles who strive for all these things; and indeed your heavenly Father knows that you need all these things.'

'Strive first for the kingdom of God and his righteousness, and all these things will be given to you as well.'

'So do not worry about tomorrow, for tomorrow will bring worries of its own. Today's trouble is enough for today.'

7   'Why do you see the speck in your neighbour's eye, but do not notice the log in your own eye? Or how can you say to your neighbour, "Let me take the speck out of your eye", while the log is in your own eye? You hypocrite, first take the log out of your own eye, and then you will see clearly to take the speck out of your neighbour's eye.'

'Do not give what is holy to dogs; and do not throw your pearls before swine, or they will trample them under foot and turn and maul you.'

'Ask, and it will be given to you; search, and you will find; knock, and the door will be opened for you. For everyone who asks receives, and everyone who searches finds, and for everyone who knocks, the door will be opened.'

'Is there anyone among you who, if your child asks for bread, will give a stone? Or if the child asks for a fish, will give a snake? If you then, who are evil, know how to give good gifts to your children, how much more will your Father in heaven give good things to those who ask him!'

'Enter through the narrow gate; for the gate is wide and the road is easy that leads to destruction, and there are many who take it. For the gate is narrow and the road is hard that leads to life, and there are few who find it.'

'Beware of false prophets, who come to you in sheep's clothing but inwardly are ravenous wolves. You will know them by their fruits.'

'Are grapes gathered from thorns, or figs from thistles? In the same way, every good tree bears good fruit, but the bad tree bears bad fruit. A good tree cannot bear bad fruit, nor can a bad tree bear good fruit. Every tree that does not bear good fruit is cut down and thrown into the fire.'

'Not everyone who says to me, "Lord, Lord", will enter the kingdom of heaven, but only one who does the will of my Father in heaven.'

'On that day many will say to me, "Lord, Lord, did we not prophesy in your name, and cast out demons in your name, and do many deeds of power in your name?" Then I will declare to them: I never knew you; go away from me, you evildoers.'

'Everyone then who hears these words of mine and acts on them will be like a wise man who built his house on rock. The rain fell, the floods came, and the winds blew and beat on that house, but it did not fall, because it had been founded on rock.'

'Everyone who hears these words of mine and does not act on them will be like a foolish man who built his house on sand. The rain fell, and the floods came, and the winds blew and beat against that house, and it fell – and great was its fall!'

8   A centurion came to him, appealing to Jesus and saying, "Lord, my servant is lying at home paralysed, in terrible distress." And he said to him, 'I will come and cure him.'

The centurion answered, "Lord, I am not worthy to have you come under my roof; but only speak the word, and my servant will be healed."

Jesus was amazed and said to those who followed him, 'Truly I tell you, in no one in Israel have I found such faith. I tell you, many will come from east and west and will eat with Abraham and Isaac and Jacob in the kingdom of heaven.'

A gale arose on the lake, so great that the boat was being swamped by the waves; but he was asleep. They woke him up, saying, "Lord, save us! We are perishing!" And he said to them, 'Why are you afraid, you of little faith?' Then he got up, rebuked the wind and[18] said to the sea, 'Peace! Be still!' Then the wind ceased and there was a dead calm. They were amazed, saying, "What sort of man is this, that even the winds and the sea obey him?"

9   Two blind men followed Jesus crying loudly, "Have mercy on us, Son of David!" Jesus said to them, 'Do you believe that I am able to do this?' They said to him, "Yes, Lord." Then he touched their eyes and said, 'According to your faith let it be done to you.' And their eyes were opened.

When Jesus saw the crowds, he had compassion for them, because they were harassed and helpless, like sheep without a shepherd.

---

18.   The rest of this sentence is from Mark 4: 39.

Jesus said to his disciples, 'The harvest is plentiful, but the labourers are few; therefore ask the Lord of the harvest to send out labourers into his harvest.'

10 'Are not two sparrows sold for a penny? Yet not one of them will fall to the ground unperceived by your Father. And even the hairs of your head are all counted. So do not be afraid; you are of more value than many sparrows.'

'Everyone therefore who acknowledges me before others, I also will acknowledge before my Father in heaven; but whoever denies me before others, I also will deny before my Father in heaven.'

'Do not think that I have come to bring peace to the earth; I have not come to bring peace, but a sword.'

'Whoever loves father or mother more than me is not worthy of me; and whoever loves son or daughter more than me is not worthy of me; and whoever does not take up the cross and follow me is not worthy of me.'

'Whoever welcomes you welcomes me, and whoever welcomes me welcomes the one who sent me.'

'Whoever gives even a cup of cold water to one of these little ones in the name of a disciple – truly I tell you, none of these will lose their reward.'

11 'Come to me, all you that are weary and are carrying heavy burdens, and I will give you rest.'

'Take my yoke upon you, and learn from me; for I am gentle and humble in heart, and you will find rest for your souls.'

'My yoke is easy, and my burden is light.'

12 A man was there [in the synagogue] with a withered hand; they asked him, "Is it lawful to cure on the sabbath?" so that they might accuse him. He said to them, 'Suppose one of you has only one sheep and it falls into a pit on the sabbath; will you not lay hold of it and lift it out? How much more valuable is a human being than a

sheep! So it is lawful to do good on the sabbath.' Then he said to the man, 'Stretch out your hand.' He stretched it out, and it was restored, as sound as the other.

13   'The kingdom of heaven is like treasure hidden in a field, which someone found and hid; then in his joy he goes and sells all that he has and buys that field.'

15   A Canaanite woman from that region came out and started shouting, "Have mercy on me, Lord, Son of David; my daughter is tormented by a demon." But he did not answer her at all. And his disciples came and urged him, saying, "Send her away, for she keeps shouting after us." He answered, 'I was sent only to the lost sheep of the house of Israel.' But she came and knelt before him, saying, "Lord, help me." He answered, 'It is not fair to take the children's food and throw it to the dogs.' She said, "Yes, Lord, but even the dogs eat the crumbs that fall from their masters' table." Then Jesus answered her, 'Woman, great is your faith! Let it be done for you as you wish.' And her daughter was healed instantly.

16   Jesus said to [his disciples] 'Who do you say that I am?' Simon Peter answered, "You are the Messiah, the Son of the living God." Jesus answered him, 'Blessed are you, Simon son of Jonah! For flesh and blood has not revealed this to you, but my Father in heaven. And I tell you, you are Peter, and on this rock I will build my church, and the gates of Hades will not prevail against it.'

'I will give you the keys of the kingdom of heaven, and whatever you bind on earth will be bound in heaven, and whatever you loose on earth will be loosed in heaven.'

Jesus began to show his disciples that he must go to Jerusalem and undergo great suffering at the hands of the elders and chief priests and scribes, and be killed, and on the third day be raised. And Peter took him aside and began to rebuke him, saying, "God forbid it, Lord! This must never happen to you." But he turned and said to Peter, 'Get behind me, Satan! You are a stumbling-block to me; for you are setting your mind not on divine things but on human things.'

Then Jesus told his disciples, 'If any want to become my followers, let them deny themselves and take up their cross and follow me. For those who want to save their life will lose it, and those who lose their life for my sake will find it.'

'For what will it profit someone to gain the whole world but forfeit his life? Or what will someone give in return for that life?'

17 Jesus took with him Peter and James and his brother John and led them up a high mountain, by themselves. And he was transfigured before them, and his face shone like the sun, and his clothes became dazzling white.

Suddenly a bright cloud overshadowed them, and from the cloud a voice said, 'This is my Son, the Beloved; with him I am well pleased; listen to him!'

When the disciples heard this, they fell to the ground and were overcome by fear. But Jesus came and touched them, saying, 'Get up and do not be afraid.' And when they looked up, they saw no one except Jesus himself alone.

18 'Truly I tell you, if two of you agree on earth about anything you ask, it will be done for you by my Father in heaven. For where two or three are gathered in my name, I am there among them.'

Then Peter came and said to him, "Lord, if my brother or sister sins against me, how often should I forgive? As many as seven times?" Jesus said to him, 'Not seven times, but, I tell you, seventy-seven times.'

19 Someone came to Jesus and said, "Teacher, what good deed must I do to have eternal life?" And he said to him, 'Why do you ask me about what is good? There is only one who is good. If you wish to enter into life, keep the commandments.' He said to him, "Which ones?" And Jesus said, 'You shall not murder; You shall not commit

adultery; You shall not steal; You shall not bear false witness; Honour your father and mother; also, You shall love your neighbour as yourself.' The young man said to him, "I have kept all these; what do I still lack?" Jesus said to him, 'If you wish to be perfect, go, sell your possessions, and give the money to the poor, and you will have treasure in heaven; then come, follow me.' When the young man heard this word, he went away grieving, for he had many possessions.

Then Jesus said to his disciples, 'Truly I tell you, it will be hard for a rich person to enter the kingdom of heaven. Again I tell you, it is easier for a camel to go through the eye of a needle than for someone who is rich to enter the kingdom of God.' When the disciples heard this, they were greatly astounded and said, "Then who can be saved?" But Jesus looked at them and said, 'For mortals it is impossible, but for God all things are possible.'

20   Two blind men [were] sitting by the roadside. When they heard that Jesus was passing by, they shouted, "Lord, have mercy on us, Son of David!" The crowd sternly ordered them to be quiet; but they shouted even more loudly, "Have mercy on us, Lord, Son of David!" Jesus stood still and called them, saying, 'What do you want me to do for you?' They said to him, "Lord, let our eyes be opened." Moved with compassion, Jesus touched their eyes. Immediately they regained their sight and followed him.

21   'What do you think? A man had two sons; he went to the first and said, "Son, go and work in the vineyard today." He answered, "I will not"; but later he changed his mind and went. The father went to the second and said the same; and he answered, "I go, sir"; but he did not go. Which of the two did the will of his father?' They said, "The first." Jesus said to them, 'Truly I tell you, the tax collectors and the prostitutes are going into the kingdom of God ahead of you.'

23   'The scribes and the Pharisees sit on Moses' seat; therefore, do whatever they teach you and follow it; but do not do as they do, for they do not practise what they teach.'

'They do all their deeds to be seen by others; for they make their phylacteries broad and their fringes long. They love to have the place of honour at banquets and the best seats in the synagogues, and to be greeted with respect in the marketplaces, and to have people call them rabbi.'

'You are not to be called rabbi, for you have one teacher, and you are all students. And call no one your father on earth, for you have one Father – the one in heaven. Nor are you to be called instructors, for you have one instructor, the Messiah.'

'The greatest among you will be your servant. All who exalt themselves will be humbled, and all who humble themselves will be exalted.'

'Woe to you, scribes and Pharisees, hypocrites! For you tithe mint, dill, and cummin, and have neglected the weightier matters of the law: justice and mercy and faith. It is these you ought to have practised without neglecting the others. You blind guides! You strain out a gnat but swallow a camel!'[19]

'Jerusalem, Jerusalem, the city that kills the prophets and stones those who are sent to it! How often have I desired to gather your children together as a hen gathers her brood under her wings, and you were not willing!'

25 'Come, you that are blessed by my Father, inherit the kingdom prepared for you from the foundation of the world; for I was hungry and you gave me food, I was thirsty and you gave me something to drink, I was a stranger and you welcomed me, I was naked and you gave me clothing, I was sick and you took care of me, I was in prison and you visited me. Then the righteous will answer him, "Lord, when was it that we saw you hungry and gave you food, or thirsty and gave you something to drink? And when was it that we saw you

---

19. These magnificent, rhetorical condemnations continue throughout the chapter and should be consulted there for a meditation on religious hypocrisy. Similarly the following chapter, about the destruction of the Temple and the end of the age, should be read as a whole for full effect.

a stranger and welcomed you, or naked and gave you clothing? And when was it that we saw you sick or in prison and visited you?" And the king will answer them: Truly I tell you, whatever you did for one of the least of these brothers or sisters of mine, you did for me.'

'Then he will say to those at his left hand: You that are accursed, depart from me into the eternal fire prepared for the devil and his angels; for I was hungry and you gave me no food, I was thirsty and you gave me nothing to drink, I was a stranger and you did not welcome me, naked and you did not give me clothing, sick and in prison and you did not visit me. Then they also will answer, "Lord, when was it that we saw you hungry or thirsty or a stranger or naked or sick or in prison, and did not take care of you?" Then he will answer them: Truly I tell you, just as you did not do it to one of the least of these, you did not do it to me. And these will go away into eternal punishment, but the righteous into eternal life.'[20]

Mark

1 Simon's mother-in-law was in bed with a fever, and they told him about her at once. He came and took her by the hand and lifted her up. Then the fever left her, and she began to serve them.

In the morning, while it was still very dark, he got up and went out to a deserted place, and there he prayed. And Simon and his companions hunted for him. When they found him, they said to him, "Everyone is searching for you." He answered, 'Let us go on to the neighbouring towns, so that I may proclaim the message there also; for that is what I came out to do.'

A leper came to him begging him, and kneeling he said to him, "If you choose, you can make me clean." Moved with pity, Jesus stretched out his hand and touched him, and said to him, 'I do choose. Be made clean!' Immediately the leprosy left him, and he was made clean.

---

20. See Mark and Luke for the passion and resurrection narratives.

2   As he sat at dinner in Levi's house, many tax collectors and sinners were also sitting with Jesus and his disciples – for there were many who followed him. When the scribes and the Pharisees saw that he was eating with sinners and tax collectors, they said to his disciples, "Why does he eat with tax collectors and sinners?" When Jesus heard this, he said to them, 'Those who are well have no need of a physician, but those who are sick; I have come to call not the righteous but sinners.'

One sabbath he was going through the grainfields; and as they made their way his disciples began to pluck heads of grain. The Pharisees said to him, "Look, why are they doing what is not lawful on the sabbath?" ... Jesus said to them, 'The sabbath was made for man, and not man for the sabbath; so the Son of Man is lord even of the sabbath.'

5   There was a woman who had been suffering from haemorrhages for twelve years. She had endured much under many physicians, and had spent all that she had; and she was no better, but rather grew worse. She had heard about Jesus, and came up behind him in the crowd and touched his cloak, for she said, "If I but touch his clothes, I will be made well."

Immediately her haemorrhage stopped; and she felt in her body that she was healed of her disease. Immediately aware that power had gone forth from him, Jesus turned about in the crowd and said, 'Who touched my clothes?' The woman, knowing what had happened to her, came in fear and trembling, fell down before him, and told him the whole truth. He said to her, 'Daughter, your faith has made you well; go in peace, and be healed of your disease.'

6   On the sabbath Jesus began to teach in the synagogue, and many who heard him were astounded. They said, "Where did this man get all this? What is this wisdom that has been given to him? What deeds of power are being done by his hands! Is not this the carpenter?"

Jesus said to them, 'Prophets are not without honour, except in their home town, and among their own kin, and in their own house.'

The apostles gathered around Jesus, and told him all that they had done and taught. He said to them, 'Come away to a deserted place all by yourselves and rest a while.' For many were coming and going, and they had no leisure even to eat. And they went away in the boat to a deserted place by themselves.

As he went ashore, he saw a great crowd; and he had compassion for them, because they were like sheep without a shepherd; and he began to teach them many things.

After Jesus had dismissed the crowds, he went up the mountain by himself to pray.[21] When evening came, the boat was out on the lake, and Jesus was alone on the land. When he saw that [his disciples] were straining at the oars against an adverse wind, he came towards them early in the morning, walking on the lake. He intended to pass them by. But when they saw him walking on the lake, they thought it was a ghost and cried out; for they all saw him and were terrified. But immediately he spoke to them and said, 'Take heart, it is I; do not be afraid.'[22] Peter answered him, "Lord, if it is you, command me to come to you on the water." He said, 'Come.' So Peter got out of the boat, started walking on the water, and came towards Jesus. But when he noticed the strong wind, he became frightened, and beginning to sink, he cried out, "Lord, save me!" Jesus immediately reached out his hand and caught him, saying to him, 'You of little faith, why did you doubt?' When they got into the boat, the wind ceased. And those in the boat worshipped him, saying, "Truly you are the Son of God."

When they got out of the boat, people at once recognized him, and rushed about that whole region and began to bring the sick on mats

---

21. This verse is from Matt. 14: 23.
22. The rest of this paragraph is from Matt. 14: 28–33.

to wherever they heard he was. And wherever he went, into villages or cities or farms, they laid the sick in the marketplaces, and begged him that they might touch even the fringe of his cloak; and all who touched it were healed.

9   'All things can be done for the one who believes.' Immediately the father of the [sick] child cried out, "I believe; help my unbelief!"

Jesus asked his disciples, 'What were you arguing about on the way?' But they were silent, for on the way they had argued with one another about who was the greatest. He sat down, called the twelve, and said to them, 'Whoever wants to be first must be last of all and servant of all.'

Jesus took a little child and put it among them; and taking it in his arms, he said to them, 'Whoever welcomes one such child in my name welcomes me, and whoever welcomes me welcomes not me but the one who sent me.'

'Truly I tell you, whoever gives you a cup of water to drink because you bear the name of Christ will by no means lose the reward.'

'If any of you put a stumbling block before one of these little ones who believe in me, it would be better for you if a great millstone were hung around your neck and you were thrown into the sea.'

10   'From the beginning of creation, *God made them male and female. For this reason a man shall leave his father and mother and be joined to his wife, and the two shall become one flesh.* So they are no longer two, but one flesh. Therefore what God has joined together, let no one separate.'

People were bringing little children to him in order that he might touch them and the disciples spoke sternly to them. But when Jesus saw this, he was indignant and said to them, 'Let the little children come to me; do not stop them; for it is to such as these that the kingdom of God belongs.'

'Truly I tell you, whoever does not receive the kingdom of God as a little child will never enter it.' And he took them up in his arms, laid his hands on them, and blessed them.

'See, we are going up to Jerusalem, and the Son of Man will be handed over to the chief priests and the scribes, and they will condemn him to death; then they will hand him over to the Gentiles; they will mock him, and spit upon him, and flog him, and kill him; and after three days he will rise again.'

'You know that among the Gentiles those whom they recognize as their rulers lord it over them, and their great ones are tyrants over them. But it is not so among you; whoever wishes to become great among you must be your servant, and whoever wishes to be first among you must be slave of all.'

'The Son of Man came not to be served but to serve, and to give his life a ransom for many.'

11 Then those who went ahead and those who followed were shouting, "Hosanna! Blessed is the one who comes in the name of the Lord! Blessed is the coming kingdom of our ancestor David! Hosanna in the highest heaven!"[23] Some of the Pharisees in the crowd said to him, "Teacher, order your disciples to stop." He answered, 'I tell you, if these were silent, the stones would shout out.'

Jesus entered the temple and began to drive out those who were selling and those who were buying in the temple, and he overturned the tables of the money changers and the seats of those who sold doves; and he would not allow anyone to carry anything through the temple. He said, 'Is it not written: *My house shall be called a house of prayer for all the nations?* But you have made it a den of robbers.'

'Have faith in God. Truly I tell you, if you say to this mountain, "Be taken up and thrown into the sea", and if you do not doubt in your heart, but believe that what you say will come to pass, it will be done for you. So I tell you, whatever you ask for in prayer, believe that you have received it, and it will be yours.'

12 [A scribe asked] "Which commandment is the first of all?" Jesus

---

23. The next two sentences are from Luke 19: 39–40.

answered, 'The first is: *Hear, O Israel: the Lord our God, the Lord is one; you shall love the Lord your God with all your heart, and with all your soul, and with all your mind, and with all your strength.* The second is this: *You shall love your neighbour as yourself.* There is no commandment greater than these.'

"Well said, teacher," the man replied. "You are right in saying that God is one and there is no other but him. To love him with all your heart, with all your understanding and with all your strength, and to love your neighbour as yourself is more important than all burnt offerings and sacrifices."

When Jesus saw that he answered wisely, he said to him, 'You are not far from the kingdom of God.'

14   When they had taken their places and were eating, Jesus said, 'Truly I tell you, one of you will betray me, one who is eating with me.' They began to be distressed and to say to him one after another, "Surely, not I?" He said to them, 'It is one of the twelve, one who is dipping bread into the bowl with me.'

'For the Son of Man goes as it is written of him, but woe to the one by whom the Son of Man is betrayed! It would have been better for him not to have been born.'

While they were eating, he took a loaf of bread, and after blessing it he broke it, gave it to them, and said, 'Take; this is my body.' Then he took a cup, and after giving thanks he gave it to them, and all of them drank from it. He said to them, 'This is my blood of the covenant, which is poured out for many. Truly I tell you, I will never again drink of the fruit of the vine until that day when I drink it new in the kingdom of God.'

'You will all become deserters; for it is written: *I will strike the shepherd, and the sheep will be scattered.* But after I am raised up, I will go before you to Galilee.'

Peter said to him, "Even though all become deserters, I will not." Jesus said to him, 'Truly I tell you, this day, this very night, before the cock crows twice, you will deny me three times.' But he said vehemently, "Even though I must die with you, I will not deny you." And all of them said the same.

They went to a place called Gethsemane; and Jesus said to his disciples, 'Sit here while I pray.'

Jesus began to be distressed and agitated. And he said to them, 'I am deeply grieved, even to death; remain here, and keep awake.'

And going a little farther, Jesus threw himself on the ground and prayed that, if it were possible, the hour might pass from him. He said, 'Abba, Father, for you all things are possible; remove this cup from me; yet, not what I want, but what you want.'

An angel from heaven appeared to him and gave him strength. In his anguish he prayed more earnestly, and his sweat became like great drops of blood falling down on the ground.[24]

Jesus came and found them sleeping; and he said to Peter, 'Simon, are you asleep? Could you not keep awake one hour? Keep awake and pray that you may not come into the time of trial; the spirit indeed is willing, but the flesh is weak.'

Again he went away and prayed, saying the same words. And once more he came and found them sleeping, for their eyes were very heavy; and they did not know what to say to him. He came a third time and said to them, 'Are you still sleeping and taking your rest? Enough! The hour has come; the Son of Man is betrayed into the hands of sinners. Get up, let us be going. See, my betrayer is at hand.'

The betrayer had given them a sign, saying, "The one I will kiss is the man; arrest him." At once he came up to Jesus and said, "Greetings, Rabbi!" and kissed him. Jesus said to him, 'Friend, do what you are here to do.' Then they came and laid hands on Jesus and arrested him.[25]

---

24. This paragraph is from Luke 22: 43–44.
25. This paragraph and the following one are from Matt. 26: 48–52.

Suddenly, one of those with Jesus put his hand on his sword, drew it, and struck the slave of the high priest, cutting off his ear. Then Jesus said to him, 'Put your sword back into its place; for all who take the sword will perish by the sword.' And he touched his ear and healed him.[26]

Then all the disciples deserted him and fled.[27]

The high priest asked him, "Are you the Messiah, the Son of the Blessed One?" Jesus said, 'I am; and you will see the Son of Man seated at the right hand of the Power and coming with the clouds of heaven.' Then the high priest tore his clothes and said, "Why do we still need witnesses? You have heard his blasphemy!"

[They] condemned him as deserving death. Some began to spit on him, to blindfold him, and to strike him, saying to him, "Prophesy!" The guards also took him over and beat him.

15 The soldiers led him into the courtyard of the palace ... they called together the whole cohort and they clothed him in a purple cloak; and after twisting some thorns into a crown, they put it on him. And they began saluting him, "Hail, King of the Jews!" They struck his head with a reed, spat upon him, and knelt down in homage to him.[28]

After mocking him, they stripped him of the purple cloak and put his own clothes on him. Then they led him out, carrying his own cross[29], to crucify him.

They brought Jesus to the place called Golgotha (which means the place of a skull). And they offered him wine mixed with myrrh; but he did not take it. And they crucified him, and divided his clothes among them, casting lots to decide what each should take.

---

26. This sentence is from Luke 22: 51.
27. This sentence is from Matt. 26: 56.
28. See John 18 and 19 for Pontius Pilate's part.
29. This detail from John 19: 17.

Jesus cried out with a loud voice, 'Eloi, Eloi, lema sabachthani?' which means, My God, my God, why have you forsaken me?

Then Jesus gave a loud cry and breathed his last … When the centurion, who stood facing him, saw that in this way he breathed his last, he said, "Truly this man was God's Son!"

16 When the sabbath was over, Mary Magdalene, and Mary the mother of James, and Salome bought spices, so that they might go and anoint him … They saw that the stone, which was very large, had already been rolled back.

As they entered the tomb, they saw a young man, dressed in a white robe, sitting on the right side; and they were alarmed. But he said to them, "Do not be alarmed; you are looking for Jesus of Nazareth, who was crucified. He has been raised; he is not here. Look, there is the place they laid him. But go, tell his disciples and Peter that he is going ahead of you to Galilee; there you will see him, just as he told you."

[The women] left the tomb quickly with fear and great joy, and ran to tell his disciples. Suddenly Jesus met them and said, 'Greetings!' And they came to him, took hold of his feet, and worshipped him. Then Jesus said to them, 'Do not be afraid; go and tell my brothers to go to Galilee; there they will see me.'[30]

Later Jesus appeared to the eleven themselves as they were sitting at the table; and he upbraided them for their lack of faith and stubbornness, because they had not believed those who saw him after he had risen.

'All authority in heaven and on earth has been given to me. Go therefore and make disciples of all nations, baptizing them in the name of the Father and of the Son and of the Holy Spirit, and teaching them to obey everything that I have commanded you.'[31]

'Remember, I am with you always, to the end of the age.'

---

30. This paragraph is from Matt. 28: 8–10.
31. This paragraph and the following sentence are from Matt. 28: 18–20.

Luke

1   The angel Gabriel was sent by God to a town in Galilee called Nazareth, to a virgin engaged to a man whose name was Joseph, of the house of David. The virgin's name was Mary.

Gabriel came to her and said, "Greetings, O favoured one! The Lord is with you." But she was much perplexed by his words and pondered what sort of greeting this might be.

"Do not be afraid, Mary, for you have found favour with God. And now, you will conceive in your womb and bear a son, and you will name him Jesus. He will be great, and will be called the Son of the Most High, and the Lord God will give to him the throne of his ancestor David. He will reign over the house of Jacob for ever, and of his kingdom there will be no end."

Mary said to the angel, "How can this be, since I am a virgin?" The angel said to her, "The Holy Spirit will come upon you, and the power of the Most High will overshadow you; therefore the child to be born will be holy; he will be called Son of God."

Mary said, "Behold, I am the servant of the Lord; let it be to me according to your word." Then the angel departed from her.

2   Mary gave birth to her firstborn son and wrapped him in bands of cloth, and laid him in a manger, because there was no place for them in the inn.

An angel of the Lord stood before [the shepherds], and the glory of the Lord shone around them, and they were terrified. But the angel said to them, "Do not be afraid; for see – I am bringing you good news of great joy for all the people."

"To you is born this day in the city of David a Saviour, who is the Messiah, the Lord. This will be a sign for you: you will find a child wrapped in bands of cloth and lying in a manger."

4   Jesus went to the synagogue on the sabbath day, as was his custom. He stood up to read ... '*The Spirit of the Lord is upon me, because he*

has anointed me to bring good news to the poor. He has sent me to proclaim release to the captives and recovery of sight to the blind, to let the oppressed go free, to proclaim the year of the Lord's favour.' He rolled up the scroll, gave it back to the attendant, and sat down. The eyes of all in the synagogue were fixed on him. Then he began to say to them, 'Today this scripture has been fulfilled in your hearing.'

All spoke well of Jesus and were amazed at the gracious words that came from his mouth.

'Truly I tell you, no prophet is accepted in his home town … [There were] many lepers in Israel in the time of the prophet Elisha, and none of them was cleansed except Naaman the Syrian.' When they heard this, all in the synagogue were filled with rage. They got up, drove him out of the town, and led him to the brow of the hill on which their town was built, so that they might hurl him off the cliff. But he passed through the midst of them and went on his way.

As the sun was setting, all those who had any who were sick with various kinds of diseases brought them to him; and he laid his hands on each of them and cured them.

5 Jesus sat down and taught the crowds from the boat. When he had finished speaking, he said to Simon, 'Put out into the deep water and let down your nets for a catch.' Simon answered, "Master, we have worked all night long and have caught nothing. Yet if you say so, I will let down the nets." When they had done this, they caught so many fish that their nets were beginning to break.

When Simon Peter saw it, he fell down at Jesus' knees, saying, "Go away from me, Lord, for I am a sinful man!" … Jesus said to Simon, 'Do not be afraid; from now on you will be catching people.' When they had brought their boats to shore, they left everything and followed him.

Word about Jesus spread abroad; many crowds would gather to hear him and to be cured of their diseases. But he would withdraw to deserted places and pray.

Some men came, carrying a paralysed man on a bed … finding no way to bring him in because of the crowd, they went up on the roof and let him down with his bed through the tiles into the middle of the crowd in front of Jesus. When he saw their faith, he said, 'Friend, your sins are forgiven you.'

The scribes and the Pharisees began to question, "Who is this who is speaking blasphemies? Who can forgive sins but God alone?" When Jesus perceived their questionings, he answered them, 'Why do you raise such questions in your hearts? Which is easier, to say: Your sins are forgiven you; or to say: Stand up and walk? But so that you may know that the Son of Man has authority on earth to forgive sins' – he said to the one who was paralysed – 'I say to you, stand up and take your bed and go to your home.' Immediately he stood up before them, took what he had been lying on, and went to his home, glorifying God.

6   All in the crowd were trying to touch him, for power came out from him and healed all of them.

Then he looked up at his disciples and said: 'Blessed are you who are poor, for yours is the kingdom of God.'

'Blessed are you who are hungry now, for you will be filled.'

'Blessed are you who weep now, for you will laugh.'

'But woe to you who are rich, for you have received your consolation.'

'Woe to you who are full now, for you will be hungry.'

'Woe to you who are laughing now, for you will mourn and weep.'

'Woe to you when all speak well of you, for that is what their ancestors did to the false prophets.'

'Love your enemies, do good to those who hate you, bless those who curse you, pray for those who abuse you.'

'Do to others as you would have them do to you.'

'If you love those who love you, what credit is that to you? For even sinners love those who love them. If you do good to those who do good to you, what credit is that to you? For even sinners do the same. If you lend to those from whom you hope to receive, what credit is that to you? Even sinners lend to sinners, to receive as much again.'

'Love your enemies, do good, and lend, expecting nothing in return. Your reward will be great, and you will be children of the Most High; for he is kind to the ungrateful and the wicked.'

'Be merciful, just as your Father is merciful.'

'Do not judge, and you will not be judged; do not condemn, and you will not be condemned.'

'Forgive, and you will be forgiven; give, and it will be given to you. A good measure, pressed down, shaken together, running over, will be put into your lap; for the measure you give will be the measure you get back.'

'The good person out of the good treasure of the heart produces good, and the evil person out of evil treasure produces evil; for it is out of the abundance of the heart that the mouth speaks.'

7   As Jesus approached the gate of the town, a man who had died was being carried out. He was his mother's only son, and she was a widow; and with her was a large crowd from the town. When the Lord saw her, he had compassion for her and said to her, 'Do not weep.' Then he came forward and touched the bier, and the bearers stood still. And he said, 'Young man, I say to you, rise!' The dead man sat up and began to speak, and Jesus gave him to his mother.

One of the Pharisees asked Jesus to eat with him, and he went into the Pharisee's house and took his place at the table. And a woman in the city, who was a sinner, having learned that he was eating in the Pharisee's house, brought an alabaster jar of ointment. She stood behind him at his feet, weeping, and began to bathe his feet with her tears and to dry them with her hair. Then she continued kissing his feet and anointing them with the ointment.

When the Pharisee who had invited him saw it, he said to himself, "If this man were a prophet, he would have known who and what kind of woman this is who is touching him – that she is a sinner." Jesus spoke up and said to him, 'Simon, I have something to say to you.' "Teacher," he replied, "speak." 'A certain creditor had two debtors; one owed five hundred denarii, and the other fifty. When they could not pay, he cancelled the debts for both of them. Now which of them will love him more?' Simon answered, "I suppose the one for whom he cancelled the greater debt." And Jesus said to him, 'You have judged rightly.'

Turning towards the woman, Jesus said to Simon, 'Do you see this woman? I entered your house; you gave me no water for my feet, but she has bathed my feet with her tears and dried them with her hair. You gave me no kiss, but from the time I came in she has not stopped kissing my feet. You did not anoint my head with oil, but she has anointed my feet with ointment. Therefore, I tell you, her sins, which were many, have been forgiven; hence she has shown great love. But the one to whom little is forgiven, loves little.' Then he said to her, 'Your sins are forgiven.' But those who were at the table with him began to say among themselves, "Who is this who even forgives sins?" And he said to the woman, 'Your faith has saved you; go in peace.'

8   'No one after lighting a lamp hides it under a jar, or puts it under a bed, but puts it on a lampstand, so that those who enter may see the light. For nothing is hidden that will not be disclosed, nor is anything secret that will not become known and come to light.'

'To those who have, more will be given; and from those who do not have, even what they seem to have will be taken away.'

Then his mother and his brothers came to him, but they could not reach him because of the crowd. And he was told, "Your mother and your brothers are standing outside, wanting to see you." But he said to them, 'My mother and my brothers are those who hear the word of God and do it.'

9 The day was drawing to a close, and the twelve came to him and said, "Send the crowd away, so that they may go into the surrounding villages and countryside, to lodge and get provisions; for we are here in a deserted place." But he said to them, 'You give them something to eat.' They said, "We have no more than five loaves and two fish – unless we are to go and buy food for all these people." For there were about five thousand men. And he said to his disciples, 'Make them sit down in groups of about fifty each.' They did so and made them all sit down. And taking the five loaves and the two fish, he looked up to heaven, and blessed and broke them, and gave them to the disciples to set before the crowd. And all ate and were filled. What was left over was gathered up, twelve baskets of broken pieces.

10 'Whoever listens to you listens to me, and whoever rejects you rejects me, and whoever rejects me rejects the one who sent me.'

At that same hour Jesus rejoiced in the Holy Spirit and said, 'I thank you, Father, Lord of heaven and earth, because you have hidden these things from the wise and the intelligent and have revealed them to infants; yes, Father, for such was your gracious will.'

Then turning to the disciples, Jesus said to them privately, 'Blessed are the eyes that see what you see! For I tell you that many prophets and kings desired to see what you see, but did not see it, and to hear what you hear, but did not hear it.'

"Teacher, what must I do to inherit eternal life?" 'What is written in the law? What do you read there?' "You shall love the Lord your God with all your heart, and with all your soul, and with all your strength, and with all your mind; and your neighbour as yourself." And Jesus said to him, 'You have given the right answer; do this, and you will live.'

"[But] who is my neighbour?" Jesus replied: 'A man was going down from Jerusalem to Jericho, and fell into the hands of robbers, who stripped him, beat him, and went away, leaving him half dead. Now by chance a priest was going down that road; and when he saw him, he passed by on the other side. So likewise a Levite, when he came to the place and saw him, passed by on the other side. But a Samaritan while travelling came near him; and when he saw him, he was moved with pity. He went to him and bandaged his wounds, having poured oil and wine on them. Then he put him on his own animal, brought him to an inn, and took care of him. The next day he took out two denarii, gave them to the innkeeper, and said, "Take care of him; and when I come back, I will repay you whatever more you spend." Which of these three, do you think, was a neighbour to the man who fell into the hands of the robbers?' He said, "The one who showed him mercy." Jesus said to him, 'Go and do likewise.'

Jesus entered a certain village, where a woman named Martha welcomed him into her home. She had a sister named Mary, who sat at the Lord's feet and listened to what he was saying. But Martha was distracted by her many tasks; so she came to him and asked, "Lord, do you not care that my sister has left me to do all the work by myself? Tell her then to help me." But the Lord answered her, 'Martha, Martha, you are worried and distracted by many things; there is need of only one thing. Mary has chosen the better part, which will not be taken away from her.'

11 A Pharisee invited Jesus to dine with him; so he went in and took his place at the table. The Pharisee was amazed to see that he did not first wash before dinner. Then the Lord said to him, 'Now you Pharisees clean the outside of the cup and of the dish, but inside you are full of greed and wickedness. You fools! Did not the one who made the outside make the inside also? So give for alms those things that are within; and see, everything will be clean for you.'

13 'What is the kingdom of God like? And to what should I compare it? It is like a mustard seed that someone took and sowed in the garden; it grew and became a tree, and the birds of the air made nests in its branches.'

Someone asked Jesus, "Lord, will only a few be saved?" He said to them, 'Strive to enter through the narrow door; for many, I tell you, will try to enter and will not be able.'

'People will come from east and west, from north and south, and will eat in the kingdom of God. Indeed, some are last who will be first, and some are first who will be last.'

14 'When you are invited by someone to a wedding banquet, do not sit down at the place of honour, in case someone more distinguished than you has been invited by your host; and the host who invited both of you may come and say to you, "Give this person your place", and then in disgrace you would start to take the lowest place. But when you are invited, go and sit down at the lowest place, so that when your host comes, he may say to you, "Friend, move up higher"; then you will be honoured in the presence of all who sit at the table with you.'

'When you give a luncheon or a dinner, do not invite your friends or your brothers or your relatives or rich neighbours, in case they may invite you in return, and you would be repaid. But when you give a banquet, invite the poor, the crippled, the lame, and the blind. And you will be blessed, because they cannot repay you, for you will be repaid at the resurrection of the righteous.'

'Someone gave a great dinner and invited many. At the time for the dinner he sent his slave to say to those who had been invited, "Come; for everything is ready now." But they all alike began to make excuses ... Then the owner of the house became angry and said to his slave, "Go out at once into the streets and lanes of the town and bring in the poor, the crippled, the blind, and the lame." And the slave said, "Sir, what you ordered has been done, and there is still room." Then the master said to the slave, "Go out into the roads and lanes, and compel people to come in, so that my house may be filled. For I tell you, none of those who were invited will taste my dinner." '

15   The Pharisees and the scribes were grumbling and saying, "This fellow welcomes sinners and eats with them."

So he told them this parable: 'Which one of you, having a hundred sheep and losing one of them, does not leave the ninety-nine in the wilderness and go after the one that is lost until he finds it? When he has found it, he lays it on his shoulders and rejoices. And when he comes home, he calls together his friends and neighbours, saying to them, "Rejoice with me, for I have found my sheep that was lost." Just so, I tell you, there will be more joy in heaven over one sinner who repents than over ninety-nine righteous people who need no repentance.'

'What woman having ten silver coins, if she loses one of them, does not light a lamp, sweep the house, and search carefully until she finds it? When she has found it, she calls together her friends and neighbours, saying, "Rejoice with me, for I have found the coin that I had lost." Just so, I tell you, there is joy in the presence of the angels of God over one sinner who repents.'

'There was a man who had two sons. The younger of them said to his father, "Father, give me the share of the property that will belong to me." So he divided his property between them. A few days later the younger son gathered all he had and travelled to a distant country, and there he squandered his property in dissolute living. When he had spent everything, a severe famine took place throughout that country, and he began to be in need. So he went and hired himself out to one of the citizens of that country, who sent him to his fields to feed the pigs. He would gladly have filled himself with the pods that the pigs were eating; and no one gave him anything. But when he came to himself he said, "How many of my father's hired hands have bread enough and to spare, but here I am dying of hunger! I will get up and go to my father, and I will say to him, 'Father, I have sinned against heaven and before you; I am no longer worthy to be called your son; treat me like one of your hired hands.'" So he set off and went to his father. But while he was still far off, his father saw him and was filled with compassion; he ran and put his arms around him and kissed him. Then the son said to him, "Father, I have sinned against heaven and before you; I am no longer worthy to be called your son." But the father said to his slaves, "Quickly, bring out a robe – the best one – and put it on him; put a ring on his finger and sandals on his feet. And get the fatted calf and kill it, and let us eat and celebrate; for this son of mine was dead and is alive again; he was lost and is found!" And they began to celebrate.'

'Now his elder son was in the field; and when he came and approached the house, he heard music and dancing. He called one of the slaves and asked what was going on. He replied, "Your brother has come, and your father has killed the fatted calf, because he has got him back safe and sound." Then he became angry and refused to go in. His father came out and began to plead with him. But he answered his father, "Listen! For all these years I have been working like a slave for you, and I have never disobeyed your command; yet you have never given me even a young goat so that I might celebrate with my friends. But when this son of yours came back, who has devoured your property with prostitutes, you killed the fatted calf for him!" Then the father said to him, "Son, you are always with me, and all that is mine is yours. But we had to celebrate and rejoice, because this brother of yours was dead and has come to life; he was lost and has been found."'

17 'Be on your guard! If another disciple sins, you must rebuke the offender, and if there is repentance, you must forgive. And if the same person sins against you seven times a day, and turns back to you seven times and says, "I repent", you must forgive.'

Ten lepers approached Jesus. Keeping their distance, they called out, saying, "Jesus, Master, have mercy on us!" When he saw them, he said to them, 'Go and show yourselves to the priests.' And as they went, they were made clean. Then one of them, when he saw that he was healed, turned back, praising God with a loud voice. He prostrated himself at Jesus' feet and thanked him. And he was a

Samaritan. Then Jesus asked, 'Were not ten made clean? But the other nine, where are they? Was none of them found to return and give praise to God except this foreigner?' Then he said to him, 'Get up and go on your way; your faith has made you well.'

18 He also told this parable to some who trusted in themselves that they were righteous and regarded others with contempt: 'Two men went up to the temple to pray, one a Pharisee and the other a tax collector. The Pharisee, standing by himself, was praying thus, "God, I thank you that I am not like other people: thieves, rogues, adulterers, or even like this tax collector. I fast twice a week; I give a tenth of all my income." But the tax collector, standing far off, would not even look up to heaven, but was beating his breast and saying, "God, be merciful to me, a sinner!" I tell you, this man went down to his home justified rather than the other; for all who exalt themselves will be humbled, but all who humble themselves will be exalted.'

19 [Zacchaeus] was a chief tax collector and was rich. He was trying to see who Jesus was, but on account of the crowd he could not, because he was short in stature. So he ran ahead and climbed a sycamore tree to see him, because he was going to pass that way. When Jesus came to the place, he looked up and said to him, 'Zacchaeus, hurry and come down; for I must stay at your house today.' So he hurried down and was happy to welcome him. All who saw it began to grumble and said, "He has gone to be the guest of one who is a sinner." Zacchaeus stood there and said to the Lord, "Look, half of my possessions, Lord, I will give to the poor; and if I have defrauded anyone of anything, I will pay back four times as much." Then Jesus said to him, 'Today salvation has come to this house, because he too is a son of Abraham.'

'The Son of Man came to seek out and to save the lost.'

20 [The scribes and chief priests] asked him, "Teacher, we know that you are right in what you say and teach, and you show deference to

no one, but teach the way of God in accordance with truth. Is it lawful for us to pay taxes to the emperor, or not?" But he perceived their craftiness and said to them, 'Show me a denarius. Whose head and whose title does it bear?' They said, "The emperor's." He said to them, 'Then give to the emperor the things that are the emperor's, and to God the things that are God's.'

21 Jesus looked up and saw rich people putting their gifts into the treasury; he also saw a poor widow put in two small copper coins. He said, 'Truly I tell you, this poor widow has put in more than all of them; for all of them have contributed out of their abundance, but she out of her poverty has put in all she had to live on.'

'Heaven and earth will pass away, but my words will not pass away.'

'Be on guard so that your hearts are not weighed down with dissipation and drunkenness and the worries of this life, and that day does not catch you unexpectedly, like a trap. For it will come upon all who live on the face of the whole earth. Be alert at all times, praying that you may have the strength to escape all these things that will take place, and to stand before the Son of Man.'

22 'I have eagerly desired to eat this Passover with you before I suffer; for I tell you, I will not eat it again until it is fulfilled in the kingdom of God.'

'Simon, Simon, listen! Satan has demanded to sift all of you like wheat, but I have prayed for you that your own faith may not fail; and you, when once you have turned back, strengthen your brothers.'

[Simon Peter] said to him, "Lord, I am ready to go with you to prison and to death!" 'I tell you, Peter, the cock will not crow this day, until you have denied three times that you know me.'[32]

[Later that evening the crowd] seized Jesus and led him away, bringing him into the high priest's house. But Peter was following at a distance. When they had kindled a fire in the middle of the

---

32. See Mark 14 and John 18 for the events which follow this verse.

courtyard and sat down together, Peter sat among them. A servant-girl, seeing him in the firelight, stared at him and said, "This man also was with him." But he denied it, saying, "Woman, I do not know him." A little later someone else, on seeing him, said, "You also are one of them." But Peter said, "Man, I am not!" Then about an hour later yet another kept insisting, "Surely this man also was with him; for he is a Galilean." But Peter said, "Man, I do not know what you are talking about!" At that moment, while he was still speaking, the cock crowed.

The Lord turned and looked at Peter. Then Peter remembered the word of the Lord, how he had said to him, 'Before the cock crows today, you will deny me three times.' And he went out and wept bitterly.

23   As they led him away [to be crucified], they seized a man, Simon of Cyrene, who was coming from the country, and they laid the cross on him, and made him carry it behind Jesus.

When they came to the place that is called The Skull, they crucified Jesus there with the criminals, one on his right and one on his left.

'Father, forgive them; for they do not know what they are doing.'

The leaders scoffed at him, saying, "He saved others; let him save himself if he is the Messiah of God, his chosen one!"

The soldiers also mocked him, coming up and offering him sour wine, and saying, "If you are the King of the Jews, save yourself!" There was also an inscription over him: This is the King of the Jews.

One of the criminals who were hanged there kept deriding him and saying, "Are you not the Messiah? Save yourself and us!" But the other rebuked him, saying, "Do you not fear God, since you are under the same sentence of condemnation? And we indeed have been condemned justly, for we are getting what we deserve for our deeds, but this man has done nothing wrong." Then he said, "Jesus, remember me when you come into your kingdom." He replied,

'Truly I tell you, today you will be with me in Paradise.'

Jesus, crying with a loud voice, said, 'Father, into your hands I commend my spirit.' Having said this, he breathed his last.

24 Two of [his disciples] were going to a village called Emmaus,[33] [when] Jesus himself came near and went with them, but their eyes were kept from recognizing him. 'What are you discussing with each other while you walk along?' They stood still, looking sad. Then one of them, whose name was Cleopas, answered him, "Are you the only stranger in Jerusalem who does not know the things that have taken place there in these days?" He asked them, 'What things?' They replied, "The things about Jesus of Nazareth who was a prophet mighty in deed and word before God and all the people, and how our chief priests and leaders handed him over to be condemned to death and crucified him. But we had hoped that he was the one to redeem Israel. Yes, and besides all this, it is now the third day since these things took place. Moreover, some women of our group astounded us. They were at the tomb early this morning, and when they did not find his body there, they came back and told us that they had indeed seen a vision of angels who said that he was alive. Some of those who were with us went to the tomb and found it just as the women had said; but they did not see him." Then he said to them, 'Oh, how foolish you are, and how slow of heart to believe all that the prophets have declared! Was it not necessary that the Messiah should suffer these things and then enter into his glory?' Then beginning with Moses and all the prophets, he interpreted to them the things about himself in all the scriptures.

As they came near the village to which they were going he walked ahead as if he were going on. But they urged him strongly, saying, "Stay with us, because it is almost evening and the day is now nearly over." So he went in to stay with them. When he was at the table with them, he took bread, blessed and broke it, and gave it to them. Then their eyes were opened, and they recognized him; and

---

33. See Mark 16 and John 20 for the beginning of the resurrection narrative.

he vanished from their sight. They said to each other, "Were not our hearts burning within us while he was talking to us on the road, while he was opening the scriptures to us?"

That same hour they got up and returned to Jerusalem; and they found the eleven and their companions gathered together. They were saying, "The Lord has risen indeed, and he has appeared to Simon!" Then they told what had happened on the road, and how he had been made known to them in the breaking of the bread.

While they were talking about this, Jesus himself stood among them and said to them, 'Peace be with you.' They were startled and terrified, and thought that they were seeing a ghost. He said to them, 'Why are you frightened, and why do doubts arise in your hearts? Look at my hands and my feet; see that it is I myself. Touch me and see; for a ghost does not have flesh and bones as you see that I have.' And when he had said this, he showed them his hands and his feet. While in their joy they were disbelieving and still wondering, he said to them, 'Have you anything here to eat?' They gave him a piece of broiled fish, and he took it and ate in their presence.

Then he led them out as far as Bethany, and, lifting up his hands, he blessed them. While he was blessing them, he withdrew from them and was carried up into heaven.

John

1 In the beginning was the Word, and the Word was with God, and the Word was God.

He was in the beginning with God. All things came into being through him, and without him not one thing came into being.

What has come into being in him was life, and the life was the light of all people. The light shines in the darkness, and the darkness did not overcome it.

He was in the world, and the world came into being through him;

yet the world did not know him. He came to what was his own, and his own people did not accept him.

To all who received him, who believed in his name, he gave power to become children of God, who were born, not of blood or of the will of the flesh or of the will of man, but of God.

The Word became flesh and lived among us, and we have seen his glory, the glory as of a father's only son, full of grace and truth.

No one has ever seen God. It is God the only Son, who is close to the Father's heart, who has made him known.

[John the Baptist] saw Jesus coming towards him and declared, "Here is the Lamb of God who takes away the sin of the world! This is he of whom I said: After me comes a man who ranks ahead of me because he was before me."

"I saw the Spirit descending from heaven like a dove, and it remained on him. I myself did not know him, but the one who sent me to baptize with water said to me, 'He on whom you see the Spirit descend and remain is the one who baptizes with the Holy Spirit.' And I myself have seen and have testified that this is the Son of God."

2 There was a wedding in Cana of Galilee, and the mother of Jesus was there. Jesus and his disciples had also been invited to the wedding. When the wine gave out, the mother of Jesus said to him, "They have no wine." And Jesus said to her, 'Woman, what concern is that to you and to me? My hour has not yet come.' His mother said to the servants, "Do whatever he tells you." Now standing there were six stone water jars for the Jewish rites of purification, each holding twenty or thirty gallons. Jesus said to them, 'Fill the jars with water.' And they filled them up to the brim. He said to them, 'Now draw some out, and take it to the chief steward.' So they took it. When the steward tasted the water that had become wine, and did not know where it came from (though the servants who had drawn the water knew), the steward called the bridegroom and said to him, "Everyone serves the good wine first, and

then the inferior wine after the guests have become drunk. But you have kept the good wine until now."

3 'Very truly, I tell you, no one can enter the kingdom of God without being born of water and Spirit. What is born of the flesh is flesh, and what is born of the Spirit is spirit.'

'The wind blows where it chooses, and you hear the sound of it, but you do not know where it comes from or where it goes. So it is with everyone who is born of the Spirit.'

'No one has ascended into heaven except the one who descended from heaven, the Son of Man. And just as Moses lifted up the serpent in the wilderness, so must the Son of Man be lifted up, that whoever believes in him may have eternal life.'

'For God so loved the world that he gave his only Son, so that everyone who believes in him may not perish but may have eternal life.'

'God did not send the Son into the world to condemn the world, but in order that the world might be saved through him.'

4 Jesus, tired out by his journey, was sitting by the well. It was about noon. A Samaritan woman came to draw water, and Jesus said to her, 'Give me a drink' ... "How is it that you, a Jew, ask a drink of me, a woman of Samaria?" ... 'If you knew the gift of God, and who it is that is saying to you: Give me a drink, you would have asked him, and he would have given you living water.'

'Everyone who drinks of this water will be thirsty again, but those who drink of the water that I will give them will never be thirsty. The water that I will give will become in them a spring of water gushing up to eternal life.' ... "Sir, give me this water, so that I may never be thirsty or have to keep coming here to draw water."

'Woman, believe me, the hour is coming when you will worship the Father neither on this mountain nor in Jerusalem. You worship what you do not know; we worship what we know, for salvation is from the Jews. But the hour is coming, and is now here, when the true worshippers will worship the Father in spirit and truth, for the Father seeks such as these to worship him. God is spirit, and those who worship him must worship in spirit and truth.'

The woman said to him, "I know that Messiah is coming ... When he comes, he will proclaim all things to us." Jesus said to her, 'I am he, the one who is speaking to you.'

The disciples were urging Jesus, "Rabbi, eat something." But he said to them, 'I have food to eat that you do not know about ... My food is to do the will of him who sent me and to complete his work.'

5   'Very truly, I tell you, the Son can do nothing on his own, but only what he sees the Father doing; for whatever the Father does, the Son does likewise.'

'The Father judges no one but has given all judgment to the Son, so that all may honour the Son just as they honour the Father. Anyone who does not honour the Son does not honour the Father who sent him.'

'Very truly, I tell you, anyone who hears my word and believes him who sent me has eternal life, and does not come under judgment, but has passed from death to life.'

'Very truly, I tell you, the hour is coming, and is now here, when the dead will hear the voice of the Son of God, and those who hear will live. For just as the Father has life in himself, so he has granted the Son also to have life in himself; and he has given him authority to execute judgment, because he is the Son of Man.'

6   'I am the bread of life. Whoever comes to me will never be hungry, and whoever believes in me will never be thirsty.'

'Everything that the Father gives me will come to me, and anyone who comes to me I will never drive away; for I have come down from heaven, not to do my own will, but the will of him who sent me. And this is the will of him who sent me, that I should lose nothing of all that he has given me, but raise it up on the last day.'

'This is indeed the will of my Father, that all who see the Son and believe in him may have eternal life; and I will raise them up on the last day.'

'No one can come to me unless drawn by the Father who sent me; and I will raise that person up on the last day ... Not that anyone has seen the Father except the one who is from God; he has seen the Father. Very truly, I tell you, whoever believes has eternal life.'

'I am the living bread that came down from heaven. Whoever eats of this bread will live for ever; and the bread that I will give for the life of the world is my flesh.'

'Very truly, I tell you, unless you eat the flesh of the Son of Man and drink his blood, you have no life in you. Those who eat my flesh and drink my blood have eternal life, and I will raise them up on the last day; for my flesh is true food and my blood is true drink.'

'Those who eat my flesh and drink my blood abide in me, and I in them. Just as the living Father sent me, and I live because of the Father, so whoever eats me will live because of me.'

'The words that I have spoken to you are spirit and life.'

Because of this many of his disciples turned back and no longer went about with him. So Jesus asked the twelve, 'Do you also wish to go away?' Simon Peter answered him, "Lord, to whom can we go? You have the words of eternal life. We have come to believe and know that you are the Holy One of God."

7   Jesus cried out, 'Let anyone who is thirsty come to me, and let the one who believes in me drink. As the scripture has said: *Out of his heart shall flow rivers of living water.*'

8   The scribes and the Pharisees brought a woman who had been caught in adultery; and making her stand before all of them, they said to him, "Teacher, this woman was caught in the very act of committing adultery. Now in the law Moses commanded us to stone such women. Now what do you say?" They said this to test him, so that they might have some charge to bring against him. Jesus bent down and wrote with his finger on the ground. When

they kept on questioning him, he straightened up and said to them, 'Let anyone among you who is without sin be the first to throw a stone at her.' And once again he bent down and wrote on the ground. When they heard it, they went away, one by one, beginning with the elders; and Jesus was left alone with the woman standing before him. Jesus straightened up and said to her, 'Woman, where are they? Has no one condemned you?' She said, "No one, sir." And Jesus said, 'Neither do I condemn you. Go your way, and from now on do not sin again.'

'I am the light of the world. Whoever follows me will never walk in darkness but will have the light of life.'

'If you continue in my word, you are truly my disciples; and you will know the truth, and the truth will make you free.'

'Very truly, I tell you, everyone who commits sin is a slave to sin. The slave does not have a permanent place in the household; the son has a place there for ever. So if the Son makes you free, you will be free indeed.'

'Very truly, I tell you, whoever keeps my word will never see death.'

'Your ancestor Abraham rejoiced that he would see my day; he saw it and was glad.' ... "You are not yet fifty years old, and have you seen Abraham?" Jesus said to them, 'Very truly, I tell you, before Abraham was, I AM.'

10 'Very truly, I tell you, anyone who does not enter the sheepfold by the gate but climbs in by another way is a thief and a bandit. The one who enters by the gate is the shepherd of the sheep.'

'The gatekeeper opens the gate for him, and the sheep hear his voice. He calls his own sheep by name and leads them out. When he has brought out all his own, he goes ahead of them, and the sheep follow him because they know his voice.'

'Very truly, I tell you, I am the gate for the sheep. All who came before me are thieves and bandits; but the sheep did not listen to them. I am the gate. Whoever enters by me will be saved, and will come in and go out and find pasture.'

'The thief comes only to steal and kill and destroy. I came that they may have life, and have it abundantly.'

'I am the good shepherd. The good shepherd lays down his life for the sheep. The hired hand, who is not the shepherd and does not own the sheep, sees the wolf coming and leaves the sheep and runs away – and the wolf snatches them and scatters them.'

'I am the good shepherd. I know my own and my own know me, just as the Father knows me and I know the Father. And I lay down my life for the sheep.'

'I have other sheep that do not belong to this fold. I must bring them also, and they will listen to my voice. So there will be one flock, one shepherd.'

'My sheep hear my voice. I know them, and they follow me. I give them eternal life, and they will never perish. No one will snatch them out of my hand.'

'If I am not doing the works of my Father, then do not believe me. But if I do them, even though you do not believe me, believe the works, so that you may know and understand that the Father is in me and I am in the Father.'

11 Lazarus was ill, so [his] sisters sent a message to Jesus, "Lord, he whom you love is ill." But when Jesus heard it, he said, 'This illness does not lead to death; rather it is for God's glory, so that the Son of God may be glorified through it.' Accordingly, though Jesus loved Martha and her sister and Lazarus, after having heard that Lazarus was ill, he stayed two days longer in the place where he was.

When Jesus arrived, he found that Lazarus had already been in the tomb for four days … When Martha heard that Jesus was coming, she went and met him, while Mary stayed at home. Martha said to Jesus, "Lord, if you had been here, my brother would not have died. But even now I know that God will give you whatever you ask of him." Jesus said to her, 'Your brother will rise again.' Martha said to him, "I know that he will rise again in the resurrection on the last day." Jesus said to her, 'I am the resurrection and the life. Those who believe in me, even though they die, will live, and everyone who lives and believes in me will never die. Do you believe this?' She said to him, "Yes, Lord, I believe that you are the Messiah, the Son of God, the one coming into the world."

When Mary [her sister] came where Jesus was and saw him, she knelt at his feet and said to him, "Lord, if you had been here, my brother would not have died." When Jesus saw her weeping, and the Jews who came with her also weeping, he was greatly disturbed in spirit and deeply moved.

'Where have you laid him?' ... "Lord, come and see." Jesus began to weep. So the Jews said, "See how he loved him!" But some of them said, "Could not he who opened the eyes of the blind man have kept this man from dying?"

Jesus, again greatly disturbed, came to the tomb. It was a cave, and a stone was lying against it. Jesus said, 'Take away the stone.' Martha, the sister of the dead man, said to him, "Lord, already there is a stench because he has been dead for four days." Jesus said to her, 'Did I not tell you that if you believed, you would see the glory of God?' So they took away the stone. And Jesus looked upwards and said, 'Father, I thank you for having heard me. I knew that you always hear me, but I have said this for the sake of the crowd standing here, so that they may believe that you sent me.' When he had said this, he cried with a loud voice, 'Lazarus, come out!' The dead man came out, his hands and feet bound with strips of cloth, and his face wrapped in a cloth. Jesus said to them, 'Unbind him, and let him go.'

12   'The hour has come for the Son of Man to be glorified. Very truly, I tell you, unless a grain of wheat falls into the earth and dies, it remains just a single grain; but if it dies, it bears much fruit.'

'Those who love their life lose it, and those who hate their life in this world will keep it for eternal life.'

Then Jesus cried aloud: 'Whoever believes in me believes not in me but in him who sent me. And whoever sees me sees him who sent me.'

'I have come as light into the world, so that everyone who believes in me should not remain in the darkness. I do not judge anyone who hears my words and does not keep them, for I came not to judge the world, but to save the world.'

13   Now before the festival of the Passover, Jesus knew that his hour had come to depart from this world and go to the Father. Having loved his own who were in the world, he loved them to the end.

Jesus, knowing that the Father had given all things into his hands, and that he had come from God and was going to God, got up from the table, took off his outer robe, and tied a towel around himself. Then he poured water into a basin and began to wash the disciples' feet and to wipe them with the towel that was tied around him.

He came to Simon Peter, who said to him, "Lord, are you going to wash my feet?" Jesus answered, 'You do not know now what I am doing, but later you will understand.' "You will never wash my feet." 'Unless I wash you, you have no share with me.' "Lord, not my feet only but also my hands and my head!" 'One who has bathed does not need to wash, except for the feet, but is entirely clean. And you are clean, though not all of you.' For he knew who was to betray him.

After he had washed their feet, had put on his robe, and had returned to the table, he said to them, 'Do you know what I have done to you? You call me Teacher and Lord – and you are right, for that is what I am. So if I, your Lord and Teacher, have washed your feet, you also ought to wash one another's feet. For I have set you an example, that you also should do as I have done to you.'

'I give you a new commandment, that you love one another. Just as I have loved you, you also should love one another. By this everyone will know that you are my disciples, if you have love for one another.'

14   'Do not let your hearts be troubled. Believe in God, believe also in me.'

'In my Father's house there are many dwelling places. If it were not so, would I have told you that I go to prepare a place for you? And if I go and prepare a place for you, I will come again and will take you to myself, so that where I am, there you may be also.'

'I am the way, and the truth, and the life. No one comes to the Father except through me.'

Philip said to him, "Lord, show us the Father, and we will be satisfied." Jesus said to him, 'Have I been with you all this time, Philip, and you still do not know me? Whoever has seen me has seen the Father. How can you say, "Show us the Father"? Do you not believe that I am in the Father and the Father is in me?'

'I will do whatever you ask in my name, so that the Father may be glorified in the Son. If in my name you ask me for anything, I will do it.'

'If you love me, you will keep my commandments. And I will ask the Father, and he will give you another Advocate, to be with you for ever. This is the Spirit of truth, whom the world cannot receive, because it neither sees him nor knows him. You know him, because he abides with you, and he will be in you.'

'I will not leave you orphaned; I am coming to you. In a little while the world will no longer see me, but you will see me; because I live, you also will live.'

'Those who love me will keep my word, and my Father will love them, and we will come to them and make our home with them.'

'I have said these things to you while I am still with you. But the Advocate, the Holy Spirit, whom the Father will send in my name, will teach you everything, and remind you of all that I have said to you.'

'Peace I leave with you; my peace I give to you. I do not give to you as the world gives. Do not let your hearts be troubled, and do not let them be afraid.'

15 'I am the true vine, and my Father is the vine-grower. He removes every branch in me that bears no fruit. Every branch that bears fruit he prunes to make it bear more fruit.'

'Abide in me as I abide in you. Just as the branch cannot bear fruit by itself unless it abides in the vine, neither can you unless you abide in me.'

'I am the vine, you are the branches. Those who abide in me and I in them bear much fruit, because apart from me you can do nothing.'

'If you abide in me, and my words abide in you, ask for whatever you wish, and it will be done for you.'

'As the Father has loved me, so I have loved you; abide in my love.'

'If you keep my commandments, you will abide in my love, just as I have kept my Father's commandments and abide in his love.'

'I have said these things to you so that my joy may be in you, and that your joy may be complete.'

'This is my commandment, that you love one another as I have loved you.'

'No one has greater love than this, to lay down one's life for one's friends. You are my friends if you do what I command you. I do not call you servants any longer, because the servant does not know what the master is doing; but I have called you friends, because I have made known to you everything that I have heard from my Father.'

'You did not choose me but I chose you. And I appointed you to go and bear fruit, fruit that will last, so that the Father will give you whatever you ask him in my name.'

'If the world hates you, be aware that it hated me before it hated you. If you belonged to the world, the world would love you as its own. Because you do not belong to the world, but I have chosen you out of the world – therefore the world hates you.'

'When the Advocate comes, whom I will send to you from the

Father, the Spirit of truth who comes from the Father, he will testify on my behalf. You also are to testify because you have been with me from the beginning.'

16 'It is to your advantage that I go away, for if I do not go away, the Advocate will not come to you; but if I go, I will send him to you.'

'I still have many things to say to you, but you cannot bear them now. When the Spirit of truth comes, he will guide you into all the truth; for he will not speak on his own, but will speak whatever he hears, and he will declare to you the things that are to come. He will glorify me, because he will take what is mine and declare it to you.'

'So you have pain now; but I will see you again, and your hearts will rejoice, and no one will take your joy from you.'

'The hour is coming when I will no longer speak to you in figures, but will tell you plainly of the Father. On that day you will ask in my name. I do not say to you that I will ask the Father on your behalf; for the Father himself loves you, because you have loved me and have believed that I came from God.'

'In the world you face persecution. But take courage; I have conquered the world!'

17 'Father, the hour has come; glorify your Son so that the Son may glorify you, since you have given him authority over all people, to give eternal life to all whom you have given him. And this is eternal life, that they may know you, the only true God, and Jesus Christ whom you have sent.'

'I glorified you on earth by finishing the work that you gave me to do. So now, Father, glorify me in your own presence with the glory that I had in your presence before the world existed.'

'I have made your name known to those whom you gave me from the world. They were yours, and you gave them to me, and they have kept your word.'

'Now I am no longer in the world, but they are in the world, and I am coming to you. Holy Father, protect in your name those that you have given me, so that they may be one, as we are one.'

'Now I am coming to you, and I speak these things in the world so that they may have my joy made complete in themselves. I have given them your word, and the world has hated them because they do not belong to the world, just as I do not belong to the world. I am not asking you to take them out of the world, but I ask you to protect them from the evil one. They do not belong to the world, just as I do not belong to the world.'

'I ask not only on behalf of these, but also on behalf of those who will believe in me through their word, that they may all be one. As you, Father, are in me and I am in you, may they also be in us, so that the world may believe that you have sent me.'

'Father, I desire that those also, whom you have given me, may be with me where I am, to see my glory, which you have given me because you loved me before the foundation of the world.'

'I made your name known to them, and I will make it known, so that the love with which you have loved me may be in them, and I in them.'

18   Judas brought a detachment of soldiers together with police from the chief priests and the Pharisees, and they came there with lanterns and torches and weapons. [Jesus asked] 'For whom are you looking?' They answered, "Jesus of Nazareth." 'I am he.' Judas, who betrayed him, was standing with them. When Jesus said to them, 'I am he', they stepped back and fell to the ground.

[Pilate] summoned Jesus, and asked him, "Are you the King of the Jews?" Jesus answered, 'Do you ask this on your own, or did others tell you about me?' Pilate replied, "I am not a Jew, am I? Your own nation and the chief priests have handed you over to me. What have you done?" Jesus answered, 'My kingdom is not from this world. If my kingdom were from this world, my followers would be fighting to keep me from being handed over to the Jews. But as it is, my kingdom is not from here.'

Pilate asked him, "So you are a king?" Jesus answered, 'You say that I am a king. For this I was born, and for this I came into the world, to testify to the truth. Everyone who belongs to the truth listens to my voice.' Pilate asked him, "What is truth?"

19 Pilate took Jesus and had him flogged. And the soldiers wove a crown of thorns and put it on his head, and they dressed him in a purple robe. They kept coming up to him, saying, "Hail, King of the Jews!" and striking him on the face.

Pilate went out again and said to [the people], "Look, I am bringing him out to you to let you know that I find no case against him." So Jesus came out, wearing the crown of thorns and the purple robe. Pilate said to them, "Here is the man!" When the chief priests and the police saw him, they shouted, "Crucify him! Crucify him!" Pilate said to them, "Take him yourselves and crucify him; I find no case against him." The Jews answered him, "We have a law, and according to that law he ought to die because he has claimed to be the Son of God."

Standing near the cross of Jesus were his mother, and his mother's sister, Mary the wife of Clopas, and Mary Magdalene. When Jesus saw his mother and the disciple whom he loved standing beside her, he said to his mother, 'Woman, here is your son.' Then he said to the disciple, 'Here is your mother.' And from that hour the disciple took her into his own home.

After this, when Jesus knew that all was now finished, he said (in order to fulfil the scripture), 'I am thirsty.' A jar full of sour wine was standing there. So they put a sponge full of the wine on a branch of hyssop and held it to his mouth. When Jesus had received the wine, he said, 'It is finished.' Then he bowed his head and gave up his spirit.

20 Early on the first day of the week, while it was still dark, Mary Magdalene came to the tomb and saw that the stone had been removed from the tomb. So she ran and went to Simon Peter and the other disciple, the one whom Jesus loved, and said to them,

"They have taken the Lord out of the tomb, and we do not know where they have laid him."

Mary [Magdalene] stood weeping outside the tomb. As she wept, she bent over to look into the tomb; and she saw two angels [who] said to her, "Woman, why are you weeping?" "They have taken away my Lord, and I do not know where they have laid him." When she had said this, she turned round and saw Jesus standing there, but she did not know that it was Jesus.

Jesus said to her, 'Woman, why are you weeping? For whom are you looking?' Supposing him to be the gardener, she said to him, "Sir, if you have carried him away, tell me where you have laid him, and I will take him away." Jesus said to her, 'Mary!' She turned and said to him in Hebrew, "Rabbouni!" (which means Teacher). Jesus said to her, 'Do not hold on to me, because I have not yet ascended to the Father. But go to my brothers and say to them: I am ascending to my Father and your Father, to my God and your God.'

When it was evening on that day, the first day of the week, and the doors of the house where the disciples had met were locked for fear of the Jews, Jesus came and stood among them and said, 'Peace be with you.' After he said this, he showed them his hands and his side. Then the disciples rejoiced when they saw the Lord.

Jesus said to them again, 'Peace be with you. As the Father has sent me, so I send you.' When he had said this, he breathed on them and said to them, 'Receive the Holy Spirit. If you forgive the sins of any, they are forgiven them; if you retain the sins of any, they are retained.'

[Thomas] was not with them when Jesus came. So the other disciples told him, "We have seen the Lord." But he said to them, "Unless I see the mark of the nails in his hands, and put my finger in the mark of the nails and my hand in his side, I will not believe."

A week later … Jesus came and stood among them and said, 'Peace be with you.' Then he said to Thomas, 'Put your finger here and see my hands. Reach out your hand and put it in my side. Do not doubt but believe.' Thomas answered him, "My Lord and my God!" Jesus said to him, 'Have you believed because you have seen me? Blessed are those who have not seen and yet have come to believe.'

21 [On another occasion the disciples] went out and got into the boat [to fish], but that night they caught nothing. Just after daybreak, Jesus stood on the beach; but the disciples did not know that it was Jesus. He said to them, 'Children, you have no fish, have you?' They answered him, "No." 'Cast the net to the right side of the boat, and you will find some.' So they cast it, and now they were not able to haul it in because there were so many fish. That disciple whom Jesus loved said to Peter, "It is the Lord!"

When they had gone ashore, they saw a charcoal fire there, with fish on it, and bread. Jesus said to them, 'Bring some of the fish that you have just caught.' So Simon Peter went aboard and hauled the net ashore, full of large fish, a hundred and fifty-three of them; and though there were so many, the net was not torn. Jesus said to them, 'Come and have breakfast.'

When they had finished breakfast, Jesus said to Simon Peter, 'Simon son of John, do you love me more than these?' He said to him, "Yes, Lord; you know that I love you." Jesus said to him, 'Feed my lambs.' A second time he said to him, 'Simon son of John, do you love me?' He said to him, "Yes, Lord; you know that I love you." Jesus said to him, 'Tend my sheep.' He said to him the third time, 'Simon son of John, do you love me?' Peter felt hurt because he said to him the third time, 'Do you love me?' And he said to him, "Lord, you know everything; you know that I love you." Jesus said to him, 'Feed my sheep.'

There are also many other things that Jesus did; if every one of them were written down, I suppose that the world itself could not contain the books that would be written.

Acts

1 [The apostles] were constantly devoting themselves to prayer, together with certain women, including Mary the mother of Jesus, as well as his brothers.

2 When the day of Pentecost had come, they were all together in one place. And suddenly from heaven there came a sound like the rush of a violent wind, and it filled the entire house where they were sitting.

Divided tongues, as of fire, appeared among them, and a tongue rested on each of them. All of them were filled with the Holy Spirit and began to speak in other languages, as the Spirit gave them ability.

[Peter said: "Jesus of Nazareth], handed over to you according to the definite plan and foreknowledge of God, you crucified and killed by the hands of those outside the law. But God raised him up, having freed him from death, because it was impossible for him to be held in its power."

"This Jesus God raised up, and of that all of us are witnesses. Being therefore exalted at the right hand of God, and having received from the Father the promise of the Holy Spirit, he has poured out this that you both see and hear."

"Therefore let the entire house of Israel know with certainty that God has made him both Lord and Messiah, this Jesus whom you crucified."

When they heard this, they were cut to the heart and said to Peter and to the other apostles, "Brothers, what should we do?" Peter said to them, "Repent, and be baptized every one of you in the name of Jesus Christ so that your sins may be forgiven; and you will receive the gift of the Holy Spirit. For the promise is for you, for your children, and for all who are far away, everyone whom the Lord our God calls to him."

Those who welcomed his message were baptized, and that day about three thousand persons were added. They devoted themselves to the apostles' teaching and fellowship, to the breaking of bread and the prayers.

Awe came upon everyone, because many wonders and signs were being done by the apostles. All who believed were together and had all things in common; they would sell their possessions and goods and distribute the proceeds to all, as any had need.

3   When [the lame man] saw Peter and John about to go into the temple, he asked them for alms. Peter looked intently at him, as did John, and said, "Look at us." And he fixed his attention on them, expecting to receive something from them. But Peter said, "I have no silver or gold, but what I have I give you; in the name of Jesus Christ of Nazareth, stand up and walk." And he took him by the right hand and raised him up; and immediately his feet and ankles were made strong. Jumping up, he stood and began to walk, and he entered the temple with them, walking and leaping and praising God.

5   [The people] even carried out the sick into the streets, and laid them on cots and mats, in order that Peter's shadow might fall on some of them as he came by.

The high priest questioned [the apostles], "We gave you strict orders not to teach in this name, yet here you have filled Jerusalem with your teaching and you are determined to bring this man's blood on us." They replied: "We must obey God rather than any human authority. The God of our ancestors raised up Jesus, whom you had killed by hanging him on a tree. God exalted him at his right hand as Leader and Saviour, so that he might give repentance to Israel and forgiveness of sins. And we are witnesses to these things, and so is the Holy Spirit whom God has given to those who obey him."

9   As Saul was going along and approaching Damascus, suddenly a light from heaven flashed around him. He fell to the ground and heard a voice saying to him, 'Saul, Saul, why do you persecute me?' He asked, "Who are you, Lord?" The reply came, 'I am Jesus,

whom you are persecuting. But get up and enter the city, and you will be told what you are to do. ...[34] I will rescue you from your people and from the Gentiles – to whom I am sending you to open their eyes so that they may turn from darkness to light and from the power of Satan to God, so that they may receive forgiveness of sins and a place among those who are sanctified by faith in me.'

10   Peter went up on the roof to pray. He became hungry and wanted something to eat; and while it was being prepared, he fell into a trance. He saw the heaven opened and something like a large sheet coming down, being lowered to the ground by its four corners. In it were all kinds of four-footed creatures and reptiles and birds of the air. Then he heard a voice saying, 'Get up, Peter; kill and eat.' But Peter said, "By no means, Lord; for I have never eaten anything that is profane or unclean." ... 'What God has made clean, you must not call profane.'

[Peter said to Cornelius and his friends] "You yourselves know that it is unlawful for a Jew to associate with or to visit a Gentile; but God has shown me that I should not call anyone profane or unclean. So when I was sent for, I came without objection ... I truly understand that God shows no partiality, but in every nation anyone who fears him and does what is right is acceptable to him."

While Peter was still speaking, the Holy Spirit fell upon all who heard the word. The circumcised believers who had come with Peter were astounded that the gift of the Holy Spirit had been poured out even on the Gentiles, for they heard them speaking in tongues and extolling God. Then Peter said, "Can anyone withhold the water for baptizing these people who have received the Holy Spirit just as we have?" So he ordered them to be baptized in the name of Jesus Christ.

---

34.   There are three accounts of the conversion of St Paul in Acts. The following sentence, from chapter 26, vv. 17–18, add interesting details to the story.

17 Paul stood in front of the Areopagus and said, "Athenians, I see how extremely religious you are in every way. For as I went through the city and looked carefully at the objects of your worship, I found among them an altar with the inscription, *To an unknown god*. What therefore you worship as unknown, this I proclaim to you. The God who made the world and everything in it, he who is Lord of heaven and earth, does not live in shrines made by human hands, nor is he served by human hands, as though he needed anything, since he himself gives to all mortals life and breath and all things. From one ancestor he made all nations to inhabit the whole earth, and he allotted the times of their existence and the boundaries of the places where they would live, so that they would search for God and perhaps grope for him and find him — though indeed he is not far from each one of us. For in him we live and move and have our being."

5. LETTERS:
Words as Communication and Connection

The New Testament's twenty-one epistles are letters (mostly attributed to St Paul) written to different communities, in which the author aims to inspire, encourage, criticize, answer questions raised and generally sort out issues both sublime and mundane. There is much that is completely up to date and totally relevant to concerns in the twenty-first century; there are points that were purely local, even at the time they were written; and there are other issues (indeed two of the most central ones for Paul) which are obsolete. Paul appears to have believed that Jesus would return again in the flesh during the lifetimes of those to whom he was writing, and this colours many of his comments; and his primary, pastoral concern was that followers of Christ need no longer follow the Jewish law, particularly regarding circumcision and dietary regulations. Paul is important as a threefold link: he was proud to be one of the chosen people of the old Covenant; he felt he was specially called to preach to the Gentiles throughout the world; and, like the vast majority of Christians in history, he never saw Jesus in the flesh.

Romans

1   I am not ashamed of the gospel; it is the power of God for salvation to everyone who has faith, to the Jew first and also to the Greek.

Ever since the creation of the world God's eternal power and divine nature, invisible though they are, have been understood and seen through the things he has made.

2   Do you despise the riches of God's kindness and forbearance and

patience? Do you not realize that God's kindness is meant to lead you to repentance?

It is not the hearers of the law who are righteous in God's sight, but the doers of the law who will be justified. When Gentiles, who do not possess the law, do instinctively what the law requires, these, though not having the law, are a law to themselves.

A person is a Jew who is one inwardly, and real circumcision is a matter of the heart - - it is spiritual and not literal.

3 Then what advantage has the Jew? Or what is the value of circumcision? Much, in every way. For in the first place the Jews were entrusted with the oracles of God. What if some were unfaithful? Will their faithlessness nullify the faithfulness of God? By no means!

For there is no distinction, since all have sinned and fall short of the glory of God; they are now justified by his grace as a gift, through the redemption that is in Christ Jesus, whom God put forward as a sacrifice of atonement by his blood, effective through faith.

5 For while we were still weak, at the right time Christ died for the ungodly. Indeed, rarely will anyone die for a righteous person – though perhaps for a good person someone might actually dare to die. But God proves his love for us in that while we still were sinners Christ died for us.

Therefore, just as sin came into the world through one man, and death came through sin so death spread to all because all have sinned … If the many died through the one man's trespass, much more surely have the grace of God and the free gift in the grace of the one man, Jesus Christ, abounded for the many.

The free gift is not like the effect of the one man's sin. For the judgment following one trespass brought condemnation, but the free gift following many trespasses brings justification.

Therefore just as one man's trespass led to condemnation for all, so one man's act of righteousness leads to justification and life for all.

Where sin increased, grace abounded all the more, so that, just as sin exercised dominion in death, so grace might also exercise dominion through justification leading to eternal life through Jesus Christ our Lord.

6   What then are we to say? Should we continue in sin in order that grace may abound? By no means! How can we who died to sin go on living in it? Do you not know that all of us who have been baptized into Christ Jesus were baptized into his death? Therefore we have been buried with him by baptism into death, so that, just as Christ was raised from the dead by the glory of the Father, so we too might walk in newness of life.

We know that our old self was crucified with him so that the body of sin might be destroyed, and we might no longer be enslaved to sin. For whoever has died is freed from sin. But if we have died with Christ, we believe that we will also live with him.

So you also must consider yourselves dead to sin and alive to God in Christ Jesus.

For the wages of sin is death, but the free gift of God is eternal life in Christ Jesus our Lord.

7   I know that nothing good dwells within me, that is, in my flesh. I can will what is right, but I cannot do it. For I do not do the good I want, but the evil I do not want is what I do. Now if I do what I do not want, it is no longer I that do it, but sin that dwells within me.

I delight in the law of God in my inmost self, but I see in my members another law at war with the law of my mind, making me captive to the law of sin that dwells in my members. Wretched man that I am! Who will rescue me from this body of death? Thanks be to God through Jesus Christ our Lord!

8   There is therefore now no condemnation for those who are in Christ Jesus. For the law of the Spirit of life in Christ Jesus has set you free from the law of sin and of death.

Those who live according to the flesh set their minds on the things of the flesh, but those who live according to the Spirit set their minds on the things of the Spirit. To set the mind on the flesh is death, but to set the mind on the Spirit is life and peace.

If the Spirit of him who raised Jesus from the dead dwells in you, he who raised Christ from the dead will give life to your mortal bodies also through his Spirit that dwells in you.

All who are led by the Spirit of God are children of God. For you did not receive a spirit of slavery to fall back into fear, but you have received a spirit of adoption. When we cry, "Abba! Father!" it is that very Spirit bearing witness with our spirit that we are children of God, and if children, then heirs, heirs of God and joint heirs with Christ – if, in fact, we suffer with him so that we may also be glorified with him.

The Spirit helps us in our weakness; for we do not know how to pray as we ought, but that very Spirit intercedes with sighs too deep for words. And God, who searches the heart, knows what is the mind of the Spirit, because the Spirit intercedes for the saints according to the will of God.

All things work together for good for those who love God, who are called according to his purpose.

If God is for us, who is against us? He who did not withhold his own Son, but gave him up for all of us, will he not with him also give us everything else?

Who will bring any charge against God's elect? It is God who justifies. Who is to condemn? It is Christ Jesus, who died, yes, who was raised, who is at the right hand of God, who indeed intercedes for us.

Who will separate us from the love of Christ? Will hardship, or distress, or persecution, or famine, or nakedness, or peril, or sword? As it is written: *For your sake we are being killed all day long; we are accounted as sheep to be slaughtered.* No, in all these things we are more than conquerors through him who loved us.

I am convinced that neither death, nor life, nor angels, nor rulers, nor things present, nor things to come, nor powers, nor height, nor depth, nor anything else in all creation, will be able to separate us from the love of God in Christ Jesus our Lord.

10 If you confess with your lips that Jesus is Lord and believe in your heart that God raised him from the dead, you will be saved. For one believes with the heart and so is justified, and one confesses with the mouth and so is saved.

There is no distinction between Jew and Greek; the same Lord is Lord of all and is generous to all who call on him. For everyone who calls on the name of the Lord shall be saved.

11 O the depth of the riches and wisdom and knowledge of God! How unsearchable are his judgments and how inscrutable his ways! From him and through him and to him are all things. To God be the glory forever. Amen.

12 Do not be conformed to this world, but be transformed by the renewing of your minds, so that you may discern what is the will of God – what is good and acceptable and perfect.

Let love be genuine; hate what is evil, hold fast to what is good; love one another with mutual affection; outdo one another in showing honour. Do not lag in zeal, be ardent in spirit, serve the Lord. Rejoice in hope, be patient in suffering, persevere in prayer. Contribute to the needs of the saints; extend hospitality to strangers.

Bless those who persecute you; bless and do not curse them. Rejoice with those who rejoice; weep with those who weep. Live in harmony with one another; do not be haughty, but associate with the lowly; do not claim to be wiser than you are.

Do not be overcome by evil, but overcome evil with good.

13 Owe no one anything, except to love one another; for the one who loves another has fulfilled the law. The commandments, 'You shall not commit adultery; You shall not murder; You shall not steal; You shall not covet'; and any other commandment, are summed up in

this word, 'Love your neighbour as yourself.' Love does no wrong to a neighbour; therefore, love is the fulfilling of the law.

It is now the moment for you to wake from sleep. For salvation is nearer to us now than when we became believers; the night is far gone, the day is near. Let us then lay aside the works of darkness and put on the armour of light; let us live honourably as in the day, not in revelling and drunkenness, not in debauchery and licentiousness, not in quarrelling and jealousy. Instead, put on the Lord Jesus Christ, and make no provision for the flesh, to gratify its desires.

14   We do not live to ourselves, and we do not die to ourselves. If we live, we live to the Lord, and if we die, we die to the Lord; so then, whether we live or whether we die, we are the Lord's.

Why do you pass judgment on your brother or sister? Or you, why do you despise your brother or sister? For we will all stand before the judgment seat of God.

15   We who are strong ought to put up with the failings of the weak, and not to please ourselves. Each of us must please our neighbour for the good purpose of building up the neighbour.

Welcome one another, therefore, just as Christ has welcomed you.

1 Corinthians

1   Jews demand signs and Greeks desire wisdom, but we proclaim Christ crucified, a stumbling block to Jews and foolishness to Gentiles, but to those who are the called, both Jews and Greeks, Christ the power of God and the wisdom of God.

God chose what is foolish in the world to shame the wise; God chose what is weak in the world to shame the strong; God chose what is low and despised in the world, things that are not, to reduce to nothing things that are, so that no one might boast in the presence of God.

2   When I came to you, brothers and sisters, I did not come proclaiming the mystery of God to you in lofty words or wisdom. For I decided to know nothing among you except Jesus Christ, and him crucified.

As it is written: *What no eye has seen, nor ear heard, nor the human heart conceived, what God has prepared for those who love him* – these things God has revealed to us through the Spirit; for the Spirit searches everything, even the depths of God.

3   I planted, Apollos watered, but God gave the growth. So neither the one who plants nor the one who waters is anything, but only God who gives the growth.

Do not deceive yourselves. If you think that you are wise in this age, you should become fools so that you may become wise. For the wisdom of this world is foolishness with God.

4   What do you have that you did not receive? And if you received it, why do you boast as if it were not a gift?

6   Do you not know that your body is a temple of the Holy Spirit within you, which you have from God, and that you are not your own? For you were bought with a price; therefore glorify God in your body.

7   The appointed time has grown short; from now on, let even those who have wives be as though they had none, and those who mourn as though they were not mourning, and those who rejoice as though they were not rejoicing, and those who buy as though they had no possessions, and those who deal with the world as though they had no dealings with it. For the present form of this world is passing away.

8   There is one God, the Father, from whom are all things and for whom we exist, and one Lord, Jesus Christ, through whom are all things and through whom we exist.

9   Though I am free with respect to all, I have made myself a slave to all,

so that I might win more of them. To the Jews I became as a Jew, in order to win Jews ... to the weak I became weak, so that I might win the weak. I have become all things to all people, so that I might by any means save some.

10   So if you think you are standing, watch out that you do not fall. No testing has overtaken you that is not common to everyone. God is faithful, and he will not let you be tested beyond your strength, but with the testing he will also provide the way out so that you may be able to endure it.

The cup of blessing that we bless, is it not a sharing in the blood of Christ? The bread that we break, is it not a sharing in the body of Christ? Because there is one bread, we who are many are one body, for we all partake of the one bread.

So, whether you eat or drink, or whatever you do, do everything for the glory of God.

11   I received from the Lord what I also handed on to you, that the Lord Jesus on the night when he was betrayed took a loaf of bread, and when he had given thanks, he broke it and said, 'This is my body that is for you. Do this in remembrance of me.' In the same way he took the cup also, after supper, saying, 'This cup is the new covenant in my blood. Do this, as often as you drink it, in remembrance of me.'

12   No one can say, "Jesus is Lord" except by the Holy Spirit.

Now there are varieties of gifts, but the same Spirit; and there are varieties of services, but the same Lord; and there are varieties of activities, but it is the same God who activates all of them in everyone.

13   If I speak in the tongues of mortals and of angels, but do not have love, I am a noisy gong or a clanging cymbal. And if I have prophetic powers, and understand all mysteries and all knowledge, and if I have all faith, so as to remove mountains, but do not have

love, I am nothing. If I give away all my possessions, and if I hand over my body to be burned, but do not have love, I gain nothing.

Love is patient; love is kind; love is not envious or boastful or arrogant or rude.

[Love] does not insist on its own way; it is not irritable or resentful; it does not rejoice in wrongdoing, but rejoices in the truth.

[Love] bears all things, believes all things, hopes all things, endures all things. Love never ends.

Now faith, hope, and love abide, these three; and the greatest of these is love.

15   For I handed on to you as of first importance what I in turn had received: that Christ died for our sins in accordance with the scriptures, and that he was buried, and that he was raised on the third day in accordance with the scriptures, and that he appeared to Cephas, then to the twelve. Then he appeared to more than five hundred brothers and sisters at one time, most of whom are still alive, though some have died. Then he appeared to James, then to all the apostles. Last of all, as to someone untimely born, he appeared also to me.

Now if Christ is proclaimed as raised from the dead, how can some of you say there is no resurrection of the dead? If there is no resurrection of the dead, then Christ has not been raised; and if Christ has not been raised, then our proclamation has been in vain and your faith has been in vain.

If for this life only we have hoped in Christ, we are of all people most to be pitied. But in fact Christ has been raised from the dead, the first fruits of those who have died.

Since death came through a human being, the resurrection of the dead has also come through a human being; for as all die in Adam, so all will be made alive in Christ.

Just as we have borne the image of the man of dust, we will also bear the image of the man of heaven.

Listen, I will tell you a mystery! We will not all die, but we will all be changed, in a moment, in the twinkling of an eye, at the last trumpet. For the trumpet will sound, and the dead will be raised imperishable, and we will be changed.

For this perishable body must put on imperishability, and this mortal body must put on immortality ... then the saying that is written will be fulfilled: *Death has been swallowed up in victory. Where, O death, is your victory? Where, O death, is your sting?*

The sting of death is sin, and the power of sin is the law. But thanks be to God, who gives us the victory through our Lord Jesus Christ.

2 Corinthians

1   Blessed be the God and Father of our Lord Jesus Christ, the Father of mercies and the God of all consolation, who consoles us in all our affliction, so that we may be able to console those who are in any affliction with the consolation with which we ourselves are consoled by God.

In Christ every one of God's promises is a 'Yes.'

3   The Lord is the Spirit, and where the Spirit of the Lord is, there is freedom.

4   We are afflicted in every way, but not crushed; perplexed, but not driven to despair; persecuted, but not forsaken; struck down, but not destroyed; always carrying in the body the death of Jesus, so that the life of Jesus may also be made visible in our bodies.

We do not lose heart. Even though our outer nature is wasting away, our inner nature is being renewed day by day.

5   If anyone is in Christ, there is a new creation: everything old has passed away; see, everything has become new!

All this is from God, who reconciled us to himself through Christ, and has given us the ministry of reconciliation; that is, in Christ God was reconciling the world to himself, not counting their trespasses against them, and entrusting the message of reconciliation to us.

For our sake he made him to be sin who knew no sin, so that in him we might become the righteousness of God.

6   We urge you also not to accept the grace of God in vain. For he says, 'At an acceptable time I have listened to you, and on a day of salvation I have helped you.' See, now is the acceptable time; see, now is the day of salvation!

9   The one who sows sparingly will also reap sparingly, and the one who sows bountifully will also reap bountifully. Each of you must give as you have made up your mind, not reluctantly or under compulsion, for God loves a cheerful giver.

12   I will boast all the more gladly of my weaknesses, so that the power of Christ may dwell in me. Therefore I am content with weaknesses, insults, hardships, persecutions, and calamities for the sake of Christ; for whenever I am weak, then I am strong.

Galatians

2   I have been crucified with Christ; and it is no longer I who live, but it is Christ who lives in me.

The life I now live in the flesh I live by faith in the Son of God, who loved me and gave himself for me.

3   Did you receive the Spirit by doing the works of the law or by believing what you heard? Are you so foolish? Having started with the Spirit, are you now ending with the flesh? Did you experience so much for nothing? – if it really was for nothing.

As many of you as were baptized into Christ have clothed yourselves with Christ. There is no longer Jew or Greek, there is no longer slave or free, there is no longer male and female; for all of you are one in Christ Jesus.

4   When the fullness of time had come, God sent his Son, born of a woman, born under the law, in order to redeem those who were under the law, so that we might receive adoption as children.

Because you are children, God has sent the Spirit of his Son into our hearts, crying, 'Abba! Father!' So you are no longer a slave but a child, and if a child then also an heir, through God.

5   For freedom Christ has set us free. Stand firm, therefore, and do not submit again to a yoke of slavery.

In Christ Jesus neither circumcision nor uncircumcision counts for anything; the only thing that counts is faith working through love.

You were called to freedom, brothers and sisters; only do not use your freedom as an opportunity for self-indulgence, but through love become slaves to one another.

The whole law is summed up in a single commandment, 'You shall love your neighbour as yourself.'

The works of the flesh are obvious: fornication, impurity, licentiousness, idolatry, sorcery, enmities, strife, jealousy, anger, quarrels, dissensions, factions, envy, drunkenness, carousing, and things like these. I am warning you, as I warned you before: those who do such things will not inherit the kingdom of God.

By contrast, the fruit of the Spirit is love, joy, peace, patience, kindness, generosity, faithfulness, gentleness, and self-control.

6   Bear one another's burdens, and in this way you will fulfil the law of Christ.

Do not be deceived; God is not mocked, for you reap whatever you sow. If you sow to your own flesh, you will reap corruption from the flesh; but if you sow to the Spirit, you will reap eternal life from the Spirit.

Let us not grow weary in doing what is right, for we will reap at harvest time, if we do not give up.

Ephesians

1   Blessed be the God and Father of our Lord Jesus Christ, who has blessed us in Christ with every spiritual blessing in the heavenly places.

He chose us in Christ before the foundation of the world to be holy and blameless before him in love.

He destined us for adoption as his children through Jesus Christ, according to the good pleasure of his will, to the praise of his glorious grace that he freely bestowed on us in the Beloved.

In him we have redemption through his blood, the forgiveness of our trespasses, according to the riches of his grace that he lavished on us.

With all wisdom and insight he has made known to us the mystery of his will, according to his good pleasure that he set forth in Christ, as a plan for the fullness of time, to gather up all things in him, things in heaven and things on earth.

God has put all things under his feet and has made him the head over everything for the church, which is his body – the fullness of him who fills all in all.

2   God, who is rich in mercy, out of the great love with which he loved us even when we were dead through our trespasses, made us alive together with Christ – by grace you have been saved – and raised us up with him and seated us with him in the heavenly places in Christ Jesus, so that in the ages to come he might show the immeasurable riches of his grace in kindness towards us in Christ Jesus.

He has abolished the law with its commandments and ordinances, so that he might create in himself one new humanity in place of the two, thus making peace; and that he might reconcile both groups to God in one body, putting to death the hostility through the cross.

3   I bow my knees before the Father, from whom every family in heaven and on earth takes its name. I pray that, according to the riches of his glory, he may grant that you may be strengthened in your inner being with power through his Spirit, and that Christ may dwell in your hearts through faith, as you are being rooted and grounded in love.

I pray that you may have the power to comprehend, with all the saints, what is the breadth and length and height and depth, and to know the love of Christ that surpasses knowledge, so that you may be filled with all the fullness of God.

4   There is one body and one Spirit, just as you were called to the one hope of your calling, one Lord, one faith, one baptism, one God and Father of all, who is above all and through all and in all.

Let no evil talk come out of your mouths, but only what is useful for building up, as there is need, so that your words may give grace to those who hear.

Put away from you all bitterness and wrath and anger and wrangling and slander, together with all malice, and be kind to one another, tender-hearted, forgiving one another, as God in Christ has forgiven you.

5   Once you were darkness, but now in the Lord you are light. Live as children of light – for the fruit of the light is found in all that is good and right and true.

Husbands should love their wives as they do their own bodies. He who loves his wife loves himself. For no one ever hates his own body, but he nourishes and tenderly cares for it, just as Christ does for the church, because we are members of his body.

Philippians

1   For to me, living is Christ and dying is gain.

2   Do nothing from selfish ambition or conceit, but in humility

regard others as better than yourselves. Let each of you look not to your own interests, but to the interests of others.

Let the same mind be in you that was in Christ Jesus, who, though he was in the form of God, did not regard equality with God as something to be exploited, but emptied himself, taking the form of a slave, being born in human likeness.

Being found in human form, he humbled himself and became obedient to the point of death – even death on a cross.

Therefore God also highly exalted him and gave him the name that is above every name, so that at the name of Jesus every knee should bend, in heaven and on earth and under the earth, and every tongue should confess that Jesus Christ is Lord, to the glory of God the Father.

Work out your own salvation with fear and trembling; for it is God who is at work in you, enabling you both to will and to work for his good pleasure.

3 For Christ's sake I have suffered the loss of all things, and I regard them as rubbish, in order that I may gain Christ and be found in him, not having a righteousness of my own that comes from the law, but one that comes through faith in Christ, the righteousness from God based on faith.

Our citizenship is in heaven, and it is from there that we are expecting a Saviour, the Lord Jesus Christ. He will transform the body of our humiliation so that it may be conformed to the body of his glory, by the power that also enables him to make all things subject to himself.

4 Rejoice in the Lord always; again I will say, Rejoice.

Let your gentleness be known to everyone.

The Lord is near. Do not worry about anything, but in everything by prayer and supplication with thanksgiving let your requests be made known to God.

The peace of God, which surpasses all understanding, will guard your hearts and your minds in Christ Jesus.

Whatever is true, whatever is honourable, whatever is just, whatever is pure, whatever is pleasing, whatever is commendable, if there is any excellence and if there is anything worthy of praise, think about these things.

I can do all things through him who strengthens me.

Colossians

1   Christ is the image of the invisible God, the firstborn of all creation; for in him all things in heaven and on earth were created, things visible and invisible, whether thrones or dominions or rulers or powers – all things have been created through him and for him.

Christ himself is before all things, and in him all things hold together. He is the head of the body, the church; he is the beginning, the firstborn from the dead, so that he might come to have first place in everything.

For in Christ all the fullness of God was pleased to dwell, and through him God was pleased to reconcile to himself all things, whether on earth or in heaven, by making peace through the blood of his cross.

I am now rejoicing in my sufferings for your sake, and in my flesh I am completing what is lacking in Christ's afflictions for the sake of his body, that is, the church.

2   When you were dead in trespasses and the uncircumcision of your flesh, God made you alive together with him, when he forgave us all our trespasses, erasing the record that stood against us with its legal demands. He set this aside, nailing it to the cross.

3   So if you have been raised with Christ, seek the things that are above, where Christ is, seated at the right hand of God.

Set your minds on things that are above, not on things that are on earth, for you have died, and your life is hidden with Christ in God. When Christ who is your life is revealed, then you also will be revealed with him in glory.

As God's chosen ones, holy and beloved, clothe yourselves with compassion, kindness, humility, meekness, and patience.

Bear with one another and, if anyone has a complaint against another, forgive each other; just as the Lord has forgiven you, so you also must forgive.

Whatever you do, in word or deed, do everything in the name of the Lord Jesus, giving thanks to God the Father through him.

4   Devote yourselves to prayer, keeping alert in it with thanksgiving.

1 Thessalonians

2   We were gentle among you, like a nurse tenderly caring for her own children. So deeply do we care for you that we are determined to share with you not only the gospel of God but also our own selves, because you have become very dear to us.

4   We do not want you to be uninformed, brothers and sisters, about those who have died, so that you may not grieve as others do who have no hope.

Since we believe that Jesus died and rose again, even so, through Jesus, God will bring with him those who have died.

The Lord himself, with a cry of command, with the archangel's call and with the sound of God's trumpet, will descend from heaven, and the dead in Christ will rise first. Then we who are alive, who are left, will be caught up in the clouds together with them to meet the Lord in the air; and so we will be with the Lord for ever.

5   Rejoice always, pray without ceasing, give thanks in all circumstances; for this is the will of God in Christ Jesus for you.

2 Thessalonians

2   Stand firm and hold fast to the traditions that you were taught by us, either by word of mouth or by our letter.

3   Brothers and sisters, do not be weary in doing what is right.

May the Lord of peace himself give you peace at all times in all ways.

1 Timothy

2   There is one God; there is also one mediator between God and humankind, Christ Jesus, himself human, who gave himself a ransom for all.

4   Everything created by God is good, and nothing is to be rejected, provided it is received with thanksgiving; for it is sanctified by God's word and by prayer.

6   Those who want to be rich fall into temptation and are trapped by many senseless and harmful desires that plunge people into ruin and destruction. For the love of money is a root of all kinds of evil, and in their eagerness to be rich some have wandered away from the faith and pierced themselves with many pains.

As for those who in the present age are rich, command them not to be haughty, or to set their hopes on the uncertainty of riches, but rather on God who richly provides us with everything for our enjoyment.

2 Timothy

2   The saying is sure: If we have died with him, we will also live with him; if we endure, we will also reign with him; if we deny him, he will also deny us; if we are faithless, he remains faithful – for he cannot deny himself.

3   All scripture is inspired by God and is useful for teaching, for reproof, for correction, and for training in righteousness, so that everyone who belongs to God may be proficient, equipped for every good work.

Hebrews

1   Long ago God spoke to our ancestors in many and various ways by the prophets, but in these last days he has spoken to us by a Son, whom he appointed heir of all things, through whom he also created the worlds.

Christ is the reflection of God's glory and the exact imprint of God's very being, and he sustains all things by his powerful word.

When he had made purification for sins, he sat down at the right hand of the Majesty on high, having become as much superior to angels as the name he has inherited is more excellent than theirs.

2   We do see Jesus, who for a little while was made lower than the angels, now crowned with glory and honour because of the suffering of death, so that by the grace of God he might taste death for everyone.

It was fitting that God, for whom and through whom all things exist, in bringing many children to glory, should make the pioneer of their salvation perfect through sufferings. For the one who sanctifies and those who are sanctified all have one Father. For this reason Jesus is not ashamed to call them brothers and sisters.

Since, therefore, the children share flesh and blood, he himself likewise shared the same things, so that through death he might destroy the one who has the power of death, that is, the devil, and free those who all their lives were held in slavery by the fear of death.

Christ had to become like his brothers and sisters in every respect, so that he might be a merciful and faithful high priest in the service of God, to make a sacrifice of atonement for the sins of the people.

Because he himself was tested by what he suffered, he is able to help those who are being tested.

4   Indeed, the word of God is living and active, sharper than any two-edged sword, piercing until it divides soul from spirit, joints from marrow; it is able to judge the thoughts and intentions of the heart.

Before God no creature is hidden, but all are naked and laid bare to the eyes of the one to whom we must render an account.

Since, then, we have a great high priest who has passed through the heavens, Jesus, the Son of God, let us hold fast to our confession. For we do not have a high priest who is unable to sympathize with our weaknesses, but we have one who in every respect has been tested as we are, yet without sin.

Let us therefore approach the throne of grace with boldness, so that we may receive mercy and find grace to help in time of need.

5   In the days of his flesh, Jesus offered up prayers and supplications, with loud cries and tears, to the one who was able to save him from death, and he was heard because of his reverent submission. Although he was a Son, he learned obedience through what he suffered; and having been made perfect, he became the source of eternal salvation for all who obey him.

7   Christ is able for all time to save those who approach God through him, since he always lives to make intercession for them.

13   Remember those who are in prison, as though you were in prison with them; those who are being tortured, as though you yourselves were being tortured.

Jesus Christ is the same yesterday and today and forever.

James

1   My brothers and sisters, whenever you face trials of any kind, consider it nothing but joy, because you know that the testing of your

faith produces endurance; and let endurance have its full effect, so that you may be mature and complete, lacking in nothing.

The sun rises with its scorching heat and withers the field; its flower falls, and its beauty perishes. It is the same with the rich; in the midst of a busy life, they will wither away.

No one, when tempted, should say, "I am being tempted by God"; for God cannot be tempted by evil and he himself tempts no one. But one is tempted by one's own desire, being lured and enticed by it; then, when that desire has conceived, it gives birth to sin, and that sin, when it is fully grown, gives birth to death.

Let everyone be quick to listen, slow to speak, slow to anger.
If any think they are religious, and do not bridle their tongues but deceive their hearts, their religion is worthless.

Religion that is pure and undefiled before God, the Father, is this: to care for orphans and widows in their distress, and to keep oneself unstained by the world.

2   Judgment will be without mercy to anyone who has shown no mercy; mercy triumphs over judgment.

What good is it, my brothers and sisters, if you say you have faith but do not have works? Can faith save you?

If a brother or sister is naked and lacks daily food, and one of you says to them, "Go in peace; keep warm and eat your fill", and yet you do not supply their bodily needs, what is the good of that? So faith by itself, if it has no works, is dead.

3   How great a forest is set ablaze by a small fire! And the tongue is a fire … with it we bless the Lord and Father, and with it we curse those who are made in the likeness of God.

The wisdom from above is first pure, then peaceable, gentle, willing to yield, full of mercy and good fruits, without a trace of partiality or hypocrisy.

A harvest of righteousness is sown in peace for those who make peace.

4   Those conflicts and disputes among you, where do they come from? Do they not come from your cravings that are at war within you? You want something and do not have it; so you commit murder. And you covet something and cannot obtain it; so you engage in disputes and conflicts.

What is your life? For you are a mist that appears for a little while and then vanishes.

Anyone, then, who knows the right thing to do and fails to do it, commits sin.

5   Confess your sins to one another, and pray for one another, so that you may be healed. The prayer of the righteous is powerful and effective.

You should know that whoever brings back a sinner from wandering will save the sinner's soul from death and will cover a multitude of sins.

1 Peter

3   Let your adornment be the inner self with the lasting beauty of a gentle and quiet spirit, which is very precious in God's sight.

Always be ready to make your defence to anyone who demands from you an account of the hope that is in you; yet do it with gentleness and reverence.

4   Above all, maintain constant love for one another, for love covers a multitude of sins.

Whoever speaks must do so as one speaking the very words of God; whoever serves must do so with the strength that God supplies, so that God may be glorified in all things through Jesus Christ.

5   All of you must clothe yourselves with humility in your dealings with one another, for *God opposes the proud, but gives grace to the humble.*

Cast all your anxiety on God, because he cares for you.

Discipline yourselves; keep alert. Like a roaring lion your adversary the devil prowls around, looking for someone to devour. Resist him, steadfast in your faith, for you know that your brothers and sisters throughout the world are undergoing the same kinds of suffering.

2 Peter

3   With the Lord one day is like a thousand years, and a thousand years are like one day. The Lord is not slow about his promise, as some think of slowness, but is patient with you, not wanting any to perish, but all to come to repentance.

1 John

1   This is the message we have heard from him and proclaim to you, that God is light and in him there is no darkness at all. If we say that we have fellowship with him while we are walking in darkness, we lie and do not do what is true; but if we walk in the light as he himself is in the light, we have fellowship with one another, and the blood of Jesus his Son cleanses us from all sin.

If we say that we have no sin, we deceive ourselves, and the truth is not in us. If we confess our sins, he who is faithful and just will forgive us our sins and cleanse us from all unrighteousness.

2   My little children, I am writing these things to you so that you may not sin. But if anyone does sin, we have an advocate with the Father, Jesus Christ the righteous; and he is the atoning sacrifice for our sins, and not for ours only but also for the sins of the whole world.

By this we may be sure that we know him, if we obey his commandments. Whoever says, "I have come to know him", but does not obey his commandments, is a liar, and in such a person the truth does not exist; but whoever obeys his word, truly in this person the love of God has reached perfection.

Whoever says, "I abide in him", ought to walk just as he walked.

The darkness is passing away and the true light is already shining. Whoever says, "I am in the light", while hating a brother or sister, is still in the darkness. Whoever loves a brother or sister lives in the light, and in such a person there is no cause for stumbling.

Do not love the world or the things in the world. The love of the Father is not in those who love the world; for all that is in the world – the desire of the flesh, the desire of the eyes, the pride in riches – comes not from the Father but from the world.

The world and its desire are passing away, but those who do the will of God live for ever.

No one who denies the Son has the Father; everyone who confesses the Son has the Father also.

3   See what love the Father has given us, that we should be called children of God; and that is what we are.

Beloved, we are God's children now; what we will be has not yet been revealed. What we do know is this: when he is revealed, we will be like him, for we will see him as he is.

Whoever does not love abides in death. All who hate a brother or sister are murderers, and you know that murderers do not have eternal life abiding in them.

We know love by this, that he laid down his life for us – and we ought to lay down our lives for one another.

How does God's love abide in anyone who has the world's goods and sees a brother or sister in need and yet refuses help?

4   Beloved, let us love one another, because love is from God; everyone who loves is born of God and knows God. Whoever does not love does not know God, for God is love.

God's love was revealed among us in this way: God sent his only Son into the world so that we might live through him. In this is love, not that we loved God but that he loved us and sent his Son to be the atoning sacrifice for our sins.

Beloved, since God loved us so much, we also ought to love one another.

No one has ever seen God; if we love one another, God lives in us, and his love is perfected in us.

God is love, and those who abide in love abide in God, and God abides in them.

There is no fear in love, but perfect love casts out fear; for fear has to do with punishment, and whoever fears has not reached perfection in love.

We love because he first loved us. Those who say, "I love God", and hate their brothers or sisters, are liars; for those who do not love a brother or sister whom they have seen, cannot love God whom they have not seen.

5   God gave us eternal life, and this life is in his Son. Whoever has the Son has life; whoever does not have the Son of God does not have life.

I write these things to you who believe in the name of the Son of God, so that you may know that you have eternal life.

This is the boldness we have in him, that if we ask anything according to his will, he hears us.

6. THE END:
After Words – After Life

The Revelation of John is written in two scripts. Some of it is chiselled in stone ... still arresting after all the centuries ... And then there is the other script: tightly written, pen driving into cheap paper, page after page of paranoid fantasy and malice.[35]

Rowan Williams's short but brilliant sermon is highly recommended for those who have struggled with this glorious, radiant, flawed, strange, frightening book – which almost didn't make it into the New Testament. Whether it is simply seen in the context of other apocalyptic (Christian and Jewish) literature of the ancient world, or instead as an earlier-dated New Testament text of central importance,[36] it can still be used for meditation on God, Time and Existence as they weave through our earthly lives and beyond. Archbishop Williams continues, later in the same sermon: 'It is madness to wear ladies' straw hats ... to church; we should all be wearing crash helmets.' That is a message which rings clear as a bell in this last book of the New Testament.

Revelation

1 Look! He is coming with the clouds; every eye will see him, even those who pierced him; and on his account all the tribes of the earth will wail. So it is to be. Amen.

'I am the Alpha and the Omega', says the Lord God, who is and who was and who is to come, the Almighty.

---

35. Rowan Williams, 'The Touch of God' in *Open to Judgement* (London: DLT, 1994) (ellipses mine), pp. 112–17.

36. Margaret Barker, *The Revelation of Jesus Christ* (Edinburgh: T & T Clark, 2000).

I saw one like the Son of Man, clothed with a long robe and with a golden sash across his chest … I fell at his feet as though dead. But he placed his right hand on me, saying, 'Do not be afraid; I am the first and the last, and the living one. I was dead, and see, I am alive for ever and ever; and I have the keys of Death and of Hades.'

2   To the angel of the church in Ephesus: 'I know your works, your toil and your patient endurance … I also know that you are enduring patiently and bearing up for the sake of my name, and that you have not grown weary. But I have this against you, that you have abandoned the love you had at first. Remember then from what you have fallen; repent, and do the works you did at first.'

To the angel of the church in Smyrna: 'These are the words of the first and the last, who was dead and came to life … Be faithful until death, and I will give you the crown of life.'

3   To the angel of the church in Sardis: 'I know your works; you have a name for being alive, but you are dead. Wake up, and strengthen what remains and is at the point of death, for I have not found your works perfect in the sight of my God. Remember then what you received and heard; obey it, and repent.'

To the angel of the church in Philadelphia: 'These are the words of the holy one, the true one, who has the key of David, who opens and no one will shut, who shuts and no one opens: I know your works. Look, I have set before you an open door, which no one is able to shut. I know that you have but little power, and yet you have kept my word and have not denied my name … Because you have kept my word of patient endurance, I will keep you from the hour of trial that is coming on the whole world to test the inhabitants of the earth. I am coming soon; hold fast to what you have, so that no one may seize your crown.'

To the angel of the church in Laodicea: 'I know your works; you are neither cold nor hot. I wish that you were either cold or hot. So, because you are lukewarm, and neither cold nor hot, I am about to spit you out of my mouth ... I reprove and discipline those whom I love. Be earnest, therefore, and repent.'

'Listen! I am standing at the door, knocking; if you hear my voice and open the door, I will come in to you and eat with you, and you with me.'

4   Day and night without ceasing [the four living creatures] sing, "Holy, holy, holy, the Lord God the Almighty, who was and is and is to come."

"You are worthy, our Lord and God, to receive glory and honour and power, for you created all things, and by your will they existed and were created."

5   Then I heard every creature in heaven and on earth and under the earth and in the sea, and all that is in them, singing, "To the one seated on the throne and to the Lamb be blessing and honour and glory and might for ever and ever!"

7   I looked, and there was a great multitude that no one could count, from every nation, from all tribes and peoples and languages, standing before the throne and before the Lamb, robed in white, with palm branches in their hands. They cried out in a loud voice, saying, "Salvation belongs to our God who is seated on the throne, and to the Lamb!"

All the angels stood around the throne and around the elders and the four living creatures, and they fell on their faces before the throne and worshipped God, singing, "Amen! Blessing and glory and wisdom and thanksgiving and honour and power and might be to our God for ever and ever! Amen."

"These are they who have come out of the great ordeal ... they will hunger no more, and thirst no more; the sun will not strike them, nor any scorching heat; for the Lamb at the centre of the throne will be their shepherd, and he will guide them to springs of the water of life, and God will wipe away every tear from their eyes."

12 "Now have come the salvation and the power and the kingdom of our God and the authority of his Messiah, for the accuser of our brothers and sisters has been thrown down, who accuses them day and night before our God."

"They have conquered him by the blood of the Lamb and by the word of their testimony, for they did not cling to life even in the face of death. Rejoice then, you heavens and those who dwell in them!"

14 "Blessed are the dead who from now on die in the Lord ... they will rest from their labours, for their deeds follow them."

21 I saw a new heaven and a new earth; for the first heaven and the first earth had passed away, and the sea was no more. And I saw the holy city, the new Jerusalem, coming down out of heaven from God, prepared as a bride adorned for her husband.

I heard a loud voice from the throne saying, 'See, the home of God is among mortals. He will dwell with them as their God; they will be his peoples, and God himself will be with them; he will wipe every tear from their eyes. Death will be no more; mourning and crying and pain will be no more, for the first things have passed away.'

The one who was seated on the throne said, 'See, I am making all things new ... It is done! I am the Alpha and the Omega, the beginning and the end.'

'To the thirsty I will give water as a gift from the spring of the water of life. Those who conquer will inherit these things, and I will be their God and they will be my children.'

I saw no temple in the city, for its temple is the Lord God the Almighty and the Lamb. And the city has no need of sun or moon to shine on it, for the glory of God is its light, and its lamp is the Lamb.

22 'I am the Alpha and the Omega, the first and the last, the beginning and the end.'

'Let everyone who is thirsty come. Let anyone who wishes take the water of life as a gift.'

Amen. Come, Lord Jesus!